THE COLLEGE FEAR FACTOR

THE COLLEGE FEAR FACTOR

HOW STUDENTS AND PROFESSORS MISUNDERSTAND ONE ANOTHER

Rebecca D. Cox

HARVARD UNIVERSITY PRESS
Cambridge, Massachusetts & London, England | 2009

Library of Congress Cataloging-in-Publication Data

Cox, Rebecca D.

 The College fear factor : how students and professors misunderstand one another / Rebecca D. Cox.

  p. cm.

 Includes bibliographical references and index.

 ISBN 978-0-674-03548-5 (alk. paper)

 1. Community college students—Psychology. 2. Community college teachers—Attitudes. 3. Teacher-student relationships. 4. Communication in education. 5. Educational psychology. I. Title.

 LB2328.C77 2009

 378.1'98019—dc22   2009016138

CONTENTS

THE COLLEGE FEAR FACTOR

TODAY'S COLLEGE STUDENTS

SMALL PRIVATE UNIVERSITIES like Harvard, Columbia, and Stanford exemplify postsecondary excellence and tradition. They provide the models for "college" on television and in film that illustrate popular conceptions about campus life and the college student experience. Harvard, for instance, symbolizes academic rigor in such films as *Good Will Hunting* (1997) and *Legally Blonde* (2001). In a recent reality show, the preeminent role of the Vidal Sassoon Academy was underscored by its description as "the Harvard of hairdressing."[1] In general, elite colleges attract a level of attention that is disproportionate to their share of postsecondary enrollments. The most highly selective universities in the United States, for instance, are responsible for only about 3 percent of the undergraduate student population.[2] Yet prospective college students yearn to attend, and the flood of applications they submit causes the selectivity of these most prestigious colleges to increase to the point that the most exclusive admit only around one-tenth of their applicants. Top-ranked public universities and elite private colleges have similarly dominated the attention of people who study higher education. Discussions about student diversity in higher education, for instance, often invoke the role of affirmative action, despite the fact that affirmative action policies apply only to universities with highly competitive admissions processes. In effect, the practices of the most prestigious universities constitute the standard for studying and assessing American higher education; other aspects of higher education are understudied and inadequately understood.

From this perspective, *The College Fear Factor* takes an unconventional approach, focusing on the least selective and least prestigious colleges in the country: community colleges. I draw on four research studies conducted over a period of five years across thirty-four community colleges and offer a frank and accurate appraisal of today's college students: their aspirations, their approach to college, and the extent to which their college experiences meet their expectations. Ultimately, this book illuminates student behavior and the classroom dilemmas that unfold at different levels of higher education, inside community colleges and throughout higher education more broadly.

Although the community college sector is often treated as an adjunct to U.S. higher education, it comprises the largest group of different types of accredited postsecondary institutions and constitutes the first stop for roughly half of today's college students. In many states (thirty-five out of fifty), enrollments are growing faster at two-year than at four-year colleges.[3] Although the community college is the bottom tier of a strictly differentiated system of higher education, it plays a central role in granting access to that system.

Since its inception at the turn of the last century, the community college has played contradictory roles. On the one hand, it has served as a democratizing element in American higher education, by enabling greater access to postsecondary study. Because of its lower cost and less selective admissions policies, the community college enrolls students who would not otherwise have attended college. To its students, the community college offers a variety of options: credit courses and degree programs that are transferable to four-year colleges, subbaccalaureate degrees and certification for a range of occupations, and noncredit adult and continuing education. For students hoping to earn some sort of college degree, three paths are possible. First, a student can transfer to a four-year college as a sophomore or junior, after taking the required coursework. Second, a student can earn an associate's degree based on transferable courses. Third, a student can earn an associate's degree in certain occupational fields without earning transferable credits. Although associate's degrees do not hold forth the same promise of economic benefits as a bachelor's degree does, they do offer advantages over a high school diploma when it comes to finding employment.[4]

On the other hand, the community college has also had a winnowing effect, in functioning as an obstacle to students who enter with the intention of transferring and earning a bachelor's degree. The high attrition rates—within individual courses and across various degree programs—suggest that students face barriers that divert them from accomplishing their goals. Studies of students entering two-year colleges with the intention of earning a baccalaureate degree indicate that these students face significant obstacles, at the level of the organization, to realizing their original aspirations.[5] Furthermore, the features that restrict students' attainment of the baccalaureate also affect students who intend to earn subbaccalaureate credentials. Indeed, scholars such as Kevin Dougherty have argued that by taking on so many, conflicting roles, the community college has imposed structural constraints on its efforts to accomplish them.[6]

The first "junior" colleges, established in California and in Illinois and other Midwestern states, embodied these contradictory impulses toward democratization of education and diversion of students from four-year colleges. Given the steadily increasing secondary school enrollments at the end of the nineteenth century, prominent university leaders, such as William Rainey Harper, president of the University of Chicago, and David Starr Jordan, president of Stanford University, worried about preserving their universities' exclusivity. Junior colleges, they believed, could accommodate the growing demand for postsecondary education, while protecting the research universities from having to meet that demand and, in turn, dilute the value of their degrees. The junior colleges could offer academic-transfer courses to the most academically able students, who would eventually receive bachelor's degrees at four-year colleges. Less able students could still gain something from the college experience—they would enter "terminal" programs designed to prepare them for the mid-skilled professions. Ultimately, the educators hoped that their universities would be able to divest themselves of the first two years of college instruction, and focus on more advanced students. That vision was never realized, but these two distinct tracks, transfer and nontransfer, remain part of the organizing structure of community colleges.

Since the establishment of those first community colleges, the college-going population has increased dramatically. At the start of the twentieth century, around 6 percent of the U.S. population graduated from high school, and 4 percent of the population attended college. Today, the high school graduation rate is close to 90 percent, and around 45 percent of eighteen-to-twenty-one-year-olds attend college. Furthermore, college going is not limited to eighteen-to-twenty-one-year-old students. Currently, around twelve hundred community colleges have over six million students enrolled in credit-bearing courses.[7] Around half of all first-time, first-semester students and just under half of all undergraduates are enrolled in community colleges.[8] Over half of all black college students and two-thirds of all Latino college students are enrolled in community colleges. In terms of both sheer enrollment numbers and the proportion of minority students, the two-year college sector has become a crucial site for higher education. From this perspective, higher education has undergone a remarkable transformation. Developed as an elite social institution, the early twentieth-century version of the university sought to prepare a select minority for leadership roles in an industrializing economy. Today, U.S. colleges claim a place as one of the most accessible postsecondary systems in the world.

The most dramatic expansion and diversification of the college-going population began during the late 1960s and early 1970s, at which point the federal, state, and local governments enacted policies intended to increase the availability of postsecondary education.[9] From 1970 to 2000, undergraduate enrollment more than doubled.[10] In large part, the expansion was accomplished through the proliferation of community colleges, which many states embraced as a viable (cost-effective) means of making higher education more available. As the number of postsecondary students increased, so did the proportion of undergraduates who were enrolled at community colleges. Thus, the expansion of higher education has produced a remarkable variety in the types of postsecondary institutions as well as diversity in the kinds of students who attend them.

This demographic diversity poses a challenge for college educators, and one of the major themes of this book is the frequent disconnect between college professors' expectations of students and students' actual performance. In some cases, professors compare their students with an idealized portrait of the college student: the person who attends college for the sake of learning, who is highly motivated and takes responsibility for his own learning, who understands the purpose of learning. More than one community college instructor, by contrast, has described her students in a way that resembles this English professor's portrayal: "The typical student has at least a twenty-hour-a-week job, which is very discouraging—it's reality, but it's very discouraging, because it cuts into *my* concept of what the requirements of a college education are; the requirements of a college education are that you devote *all* or most of your time to that—*that's* your job. And of course you get a group of kids who have no conception of what college is all about . . . who don't understand learning or the goal of learning."

Such comments seem to be a lament for the disappearance of a kind of student that no longer exists. It is not entirely clear, however, whether the ideal student ever did exist, or whether highly motivated students ever made up more than a small minority of the college-going population. One veteran college instructor mused during an interview, "It seems to me that we've been complaining about this forever, though. I can go back to when I was first hired, and people were complaining about the quality of students not holding up. So I don't know."

Indeed, complaints about students' abilities and motivation are by no means a new phenomenon. For well over a century—ever since the establishment of the modern university—college faculty members have complained about students' writing, study habits, and overall commitment to learning. Charles Eliot, the president of Harvard from 1869 until 1909, wrote a letter in which he described the typical student as follows: "The striking things about the American boy from well-to-do families are his undeveloped taste and faculty for individual labor, the triviality of his habitual subjects of thought, the brevity of his vocabulary, and his lack of judgment and sense of proportion in historical, literary and scientific subjects."[11]

At the same time, tremendous demographic changes certainly have taken place in the college student population. They have been accompanied by new patterns of attendance. The "traditional" trajectory, of enrolling as a full-time student in a residential college and attending for four years continuously, no longer represents the norm. Today's typical college student is almost as likely to attend a two-year college as a four-year college. Even when students do go directly from high school to a four-year college, they may attend two or three different colleges before obtaining a degree and take breaks or interrupt the course of study for extended periods in moving between colleges, before returning to school. To take one example, of a sampling of students who graduated from high school in 1992 and entered four-year colleges, only 52 percent attended a single college on a continuous basis.[12] Students are more likely than in the past to work while enrolled in college, to attend school part-time, and to manage work and family responsibilities that compete with school. In short, the traditional college student is no longer the typical college student.

In fact, the popular notion of the young adult who is enrolled in school full-time is outdated. Although the traditional image is a compelling and persistent one, the current college-going population exhibits a great many nontraditional characteristics, which may include financial independence, part-time college attendance, delayed enrollment after high school, full-time employment, and time spent caring for dependents. In 1999 a report from the National Center for Education Statistics (NCES) estimated that nearly 75 percent of all undergraduates possessed nontraditional characteristics and that 28 percent were highly nontraditional, exhibiting four or more of these characteristics.[13] Sixty-seven percent of the students described as "highly nontraditional" (those with four or more nontraditional characteristics) were enrolled at two-year colleges.

Given this tremendous transformation in the college-going population, it makes sense to ask whether American higher education has adapted to the changes. Are colleges prepared to educate today's students?

Key indicators suggest that colleges are *not* ready to educate today's college students. The purported accessibility of higher education, for instance, has not resulted in high levels of degree attainment; statistics on college attendance and completion illustrate huge gaps between those who aspire to earn college degrees and those who succeed. Surveys since the early 1990s have indicated that the vast majority of high school students hope to earn four-year college degrees. Of those who enroll in college with that intention, however, many end up leaving college before completing any type of degree. In fact, the proportion of students seeking a college degree (either an associate's or a bachelor's) who graduate within ten years is only slightly above half. The gap between aspiration and reality is best illustrated by the following numbers: whereas 69 percent of twelfth graders intend to earn a baccalaureate degree, only 28 percent of twenty-five-to-thirty-four-year-olds hold baccalaureate degrees.[14]

The rates of degree completion are lowest for students from groups that have historically been disadvantaged. Data from the U.S. Census indicate that whereas 35 percent of white adults aged twenty-five to thirty-four held bachelor's degrees in 2000, for African Americans it was 18 percent, and for Latinos 10 percent. Lower-income students are much less likely to enroll in college than their more affluent peers; once enrolled, the former are less likely to complete a degree. Such disparities suggest that the opportunities postsecondary degrees offer are not equally distributed across different segments of the population. The American system of providing higher education for the masses remains an unfinished project, and perhaps not surprisingly, the students who are the least "traditional" are also the least likely to realize their educational dreams.

The expansion of the U.S. postsecondary system seems even less successful when compared with that of other countries. It is true that the United States, judged in relation to other members of the Organisation for Economic Co-operation and Development (OECD), claims a percentage of adults with college degrees —four-year and two-year combined—that looks relatively high. With the exception of Japan and Korea, where over 50 percent of twenty-three-to-thirty-four-year-olds have college degrees, the United States boasts one of the higher rates of college completion (39 percent).

The United States compares less favorably to other OECD countries, however, in another regard. Although the number of college goers has grown dramatically over the past four decades, the number of college graduates has merely kept pace with the overall population growth. The percentage of adults with college degrees has undergone virtually no change in the past forty years. By contrast, other countries have increased their college graduation rates—in the case of Japan and Korea, by over 30 percent. Unlike other wealthy democracies, the United States has not enacted policies or targeted resources in ways that improve the college graduation rate of the population.

These indicators—both domestic and international—raise two critical questions. How is it that the percentage of the population with college degrees has stayed the same over the past four decades? And what accounts for the huge gap between individuals' aspirations to earn a college degree and the actual rates of college completion?

The explanation for the disparities lies in the fundamental contradiction between the elite origins of American higher education and current increased access for people previously excluded. Higher education's exclusive beginnings have kept colleges from adequately serving a greater proportion of the population, and the idealized images of college and college students inherited from the past have limited our ability to reimagine what college can or should accomplish. Fundamentally, the demographic shift in the college-going population continues to complicate the job for educators. The complications are perhaps most evident at community colleges, where the diversity of students is most pronounced, but occur at every level of higher education where students belong to previously excluded groups, including women, racial and ethnic minorities, and working-class students.

THE NEED FOR CLASSROOM-LEVEL INVESTIGATION

The most compelling evidence of this disjuncture emerges at the classroom level, in the persistent gap between the faculty understanding of college-level coursework and the kind of work that students are prepared to do. This gap, which lies at the root of a variety of classroom dilemmas, is explored throughout the book. To a certain extent, this phenomenon has been described by researchers over the past four decades. Howard London, for instance, observed the conflict inside community college classrooms in the 1970s, as working-class students resisted the abstract exercises that their professors devised.[15] In the 1980s Mike Rose documented the problem facing first-semester students at UCLA. Professors were asking the class to analyze texts, but some students were unprepared to do so, for their high school work had familiarized them with summarizing and paraphrasing, but nothing more.[16] Although they had qualified for admission to UCLA, they were unprepared for instructors' expectations about college coursework. Norton Grubb and his colleagues described the mismatch in community college classrooms in the 1990s as one in which students lacked "any real sense of how much work is expected of them in college." Consequently, "instructors confront resistance from students who literally have no idea that the demands on them are reasonable, and they face passivity from students who are used to sitting quietly through didactic classes."[17] In my research I have—for the most part—focused on students who have been deemed qualified for college-level work by reason of their scores on the math and English assessment exams yet have exhibited the same kind of behavior as students in these prior studies.

One common thread between these studies and my own research is the sense of disappointment and surprise on the part of college professors when they discover their students' weaknesses. When I asked a veteran English professor to describe his typical student, he replied, "Underprepared as far as study skills, a poor reader, poorer skill at mechanics than I anticipated. Much less skill at organizing papers and supporting and dealing with sentences and so forth."

Over the past decade, researchers and policymakers have become increasingly concerned about "college readiness." The current discourse highlighting the extent of postsecondary underpreparation attributes the problem in large part to a disconnect between the K–12 and the higher education systems.[18] A clear example of the problem appears in states like California, Texas, and New York, each of which requires students to pass the state's high school exit exam in order to receive a diploma. Yet many of the same students who successfully graduate from high school are placed in remedial courses in college, on the basis of their performance on entry-level college placement tests. The problem extends beyond the need for remedial courses, however. Even in college classes, with students who have met entry-level requirements, professors lament students' weak skills and lack of preparation for the demands of college. What it is exactly that constitutes college readiness, therefore, is not well defined.

Indeed, faculty members' expectations reflect specific assumptions about what constitutes an acceptable college student performance. Sometimes the assumptions about appropriate social behavior and academic performance are class- or race-based, embodying norms and values that are not universally held or even acknowledged. Students can easily arrive at college without understanding what is expected or how to meet the expectations. Being unprepared to meet certain expectations, however, is not the same as being unable to meet them. When students fail to follow, or even violate, rules that are taken for granted, instructors may easily misinterpret the source of the problem. If a student's style of participation is different from the norm, for example, an instructor may believe that the student is not as capable as the other students.[19] Similarly, when a student fails to take the initiative to ask questions or seek assistance, an instructor may simply assume that the student is not motivated to learn.

Particular pedagogical approaches can exacerbate the problem. Teachers who rely on conventions that are well established in their discipline may become pessimistic about their students' abilities if their teaching strategies prove ineffective. In the case of writing instruction, for instance, the dominant model for teaching, sometimes referred to as current-traditional rhetoric, has its roots in a nineteenth-century theory of writing.[20] Some of the most innovative and successful approaches to writing instruction, however, are based on a completely different model of literacy. George Hillocks's work demonstrates that community college instructors who employ less conventional approaches are both more optimistic about their students and more effective as teachers.[21] Unfortunately, in Hillocks's study, those who stuck with the established tradition and hence tended to have more pessimistic assessments of students' ability made up the majority of the faculty.

According to other studies, professors who view their students as underprepared for college tend to respond in one of two ways. One approach is to "maintain standards," by continuing along as usual, in the hope that students will learn, but with the recognition that some will not succeed. As one instructor I spoke with explained, "I haven't changed my standards. If a student is having trouble because of a job, early on, I'll say, 'Well, maybe you could switch to somebody else's class.'" Similarly, another instructor who situated herself on the side of standards noted, "Some of us are—I hesitate to say—more 'rigorous' than others. Some of us are more demanding in our problems. I give really hard problems in my classes. As far as I'm concerned, this is college. It's time you learned to think on your own. And there are students who will not take classes from me because I have a reputation as one of the harder instructors on campus. On the other hand, we do have a couple [of instructors] that they will take classes from because they're more willing to slow down for the students, which I'm not." The other common approach is to try to make the work easier, whether by slowing down, by breaking the subject matter into discrete parts, or by assigning less. This strategy, however, risks focusing on low-level cognitive objectives to the exclusion of higher-order thinking skills. As a result, this sort of accommodation can result in lowered standards and the dilution of course content.[22]

Research on college teaching indicates that successful professors are able to maintain high expectations while helping students to meet those standards. Ken Bain, in research taking into account different kinds of colleges, identified the basic features of excellent teaching—defined as teaching that results in deep and lasting learning. Among his conclusions were that excellent teachers tend to assume that their students can learn at a high level, and that such teachers understand enough about how people learn to be able to support in-depth learning.[23] To do so, however, is no simple task. It presupposes a level of pedagogical skill that goes far beyond knowledge of the subject matter or the application of generic teaching techniques. In the context of college teaching, Diana Laurillard aptly describes the basis of such pedagogical expertise as recognition of "the ways [the subject] can come to be understood, the ways it can be misunderstood, what counts as understanding: how individuals experience the subject."[24] Fundamentally, such knowledge requires a well-grounded understanding of students' perspectives, expectations, and behavior. Without that understanding, instructors are unable to accomplish their goals for students' learning. At the same time, multiple and conflicting expectations—among students and instructors—can easily lead to miscommunication in the classroom and undermine the learning environment.

In *The College Fear Factor* I examine the resulting classroom dilemmas by first focusing on students' perspectives on college, then illustrating how their beliefs and behavior influence classroom dynamics. By exploring the college experience for today's typical students *inside* college classrooms, I illustrate the importance of reconsidering higher education from within. I contend that accommodating the changing patterns of participation in higher education will require organizational changes, and that these will benefit all college students at every level.[25] But changing from within requires a more comprehensive understanding of today's college students and how to address their needs. In other words, classroom-level tensions generated by increased access to higher education suggest the need for an inside-out approach to reinventing college. Responding to the realities of today's students will, in turn, better serve the ideals of postsecondary opportunity and equity. If that is to happen, we must uncover students' preconceptions and expectations and integrate those results as we rethink course objectives and the means of accomplishing them.

The book follows the model of an inside-out exploration. The first of the three parts begins with an examination of students' goals, expectations, and orientation toward college. The second part focuses on the interactions between professors and students inside individual classrooms, and the third examines the issue of academic literacy across classrooms. As a whole, my aim is to illuminate how college students understand their educational paths, what mismatches exist between their expectations and their professors' expectations, and how some of the traditional structures and norms of higher education function as obstacles to increased access and educational opportunity.[26] Ultimately, American higher education is due for reinvention, if it is to address the realities that apply to today's students and to better address the American ideal of educational opportunity.

PART 1

STUDENTS

ONE OF THE TRUISMS about the two-year sector is that its diversity when it comes to educational missions, program offerings, and student population creates a bewildering and contradictory set of policies and practices within each college.[1] In addition, community colleges are heavily influenced by the local and state contexts, and as a result the variation extends across colleges as well. This factor complicates efforts to offer an accurate description of community colleges and the students who attend them.

Even colleges serving the same metropolitan area may have wildly different reputations. I have visited campuses that students characterize as a continuation of high school, either because the campus draws "all the dual-enrollment kids"—high school students taking college courses for credit—or because, as the intermediate step between high school and four-year colleges, it more closely resembles the high school stage than a university. In the words of a student describing his college, "This is an in-between thing; use this as a warm-up if you're not sure you want to go to a four-year." Or as another student put it, "This is like high school with cigarettes." Other colleges boast distinguished academic reputations, and I have heard students refer to a particular college on the West Coast as the sister school to the state's top university, and to a college in the Northeast as "Har-

vard on the Hill." The most vivid description I have heard requires familiarity with *Boyz n the 'Hood* (1991), a film portray-
ing the poverty and violence facing black men in the inner-city
ghetto of South-Central Los Angeles. Justifying her decision not
to attend the college closest to her home, Nora characterized it
like this: "Have you seen that movie *Boyz n the 'Hood*? Think of
the 'hood—with some classes." Most often, though, the fundamental character of the community college derives from the idea
that its doors are open to everyone. At more than one college,
students and faculty members joked that the full name of a college with initials like ACC or ECC should really be Anyone Can
Come or Everyone Can Come.

Inside different colleges—indeed, inside individual classrooms
—students may be pursuing one of many possible goals, including transfer to a baccalaureate-granting college, certification or
licensure in an occupation, exploration of possible career paths,
avocational interests, or job-specific professional development.
On average, though, well over two-thirds of first-time community college students enter with the express goal of attaining an
educational credential. With two exceptions, the students who
participated in my research were following specific degree paths.

Recent high school graduates, who represent the majority of
first-time community college students, tended to report that they
had always assumed that college would be the immediate step
after they finished high school. Such students arrived at the community college with the intention of completing two years of
coursework before transferring to a four-year college. Some arrived at the community college feeling academically prepared for
college-level work. Others found themselves there because of
their weak academic backgrounds. Mariella, for example, noted,
"I didn't have the best grades in high school, so I didn't apply to
any four-year colleges. I just thought it was a waste of time, since
I knew that I wasn't going anywhere real good. So that's why I'm
here." If inadequate academic preparation accounted for some

students' arrival at a community college, for others finances had dictated the path to take. One student characterized recent high school graduates as follows: "A lot of people who come to the community college—not half, but a lot of them—are here because they don't have the grades to get into a good college, and the other people are here because they don't have the money to get into a good college. That's my experience. Between those two things, some people coming in aren't really that dedicated and other people are; it's the same at any college" (Shelley). Mark, for instance, a second-semester student majoring in computer science, explained, "I'll be going here for a year and then transferring to [the nearby university]. I thought it would be nice to save a little money before I head off." Shelley, who hoped to transfer to a four-year college in environmental science, viewed her community college stint as the only way of being able to afford college tuition. Regarding her choice to attend a community college, she said, "Really it was just financial. I got into several out-of-state universities coming out of high school, but I couldn't afford any of them. Even with academic scholarships they were still too much money, because I have to pay for half of my own college. My parents will only pay half of what in-state would cost, and the cost of [the universities] was ridiculous, so I came here." Some of the students who delayed going to college for a few years after high school graduation asserted that college attendance was never in doubt for them, but that they needed to take a break between high school and college. In some cases, work or family obligations required their full attention. In other cases, students attributed the delay to being "tired" of school. Hugh, for example, knew when he graduated from high school that he would eventually attend college. "I wanted an education, but I wasn't ready to put forth the horsepower; I wasn't ready to get serious about it. So three years later I found myself working in [Southwestern city], and started spending time around some people that were influencing me towards getting a degree. And after about, I'd say, six months of thinking things through, I decided that I wanted to get started on a four-year degree of some sort." Other students who delayed their college enrollment after high school had not imagined that they would ever take advantage of higher education. Especially for male students in this category, the impetus for returning to school was most often economic. Paul noted, for instance, that after several years of full-time employment, "I saw what different paths my friends went on, and I decided that I didn't want to *not* go back to school at all." In particular, he said, "I saw friends working at the pizza place—and I didn't want to do that."

Jay, who also returned to school to advance his career, had for financial reasons not expected to have a shot at higher education. "My friends had the ability to go straight into university without worrying about paying. I didn't. I lived on my own in high school, and so as soon as I graduated I needed to produce money because I didn't have any."

For women who had left high school and started families years earlier, attending college had not been part of the plan. Changes in their lives, though, had spurred them to consider higher education. Often this decision coincided with their children's entering elementary school. Marie, who was pursuing a degree in social work, recalled, "At one time, [my husband] had a little problem with his health and we were at the hospital. I started to look around and said, 'I can do this,' and that's how it all began. My children are old enough so I can say, 'It's time for Mom to do something she would really like.' And that is how it all emerged: I wanted to get back to school for myself."

I could offer many more examples of the lives and pathways of individual students, but in the end I cannot tell the story of every student I have met. Instead, in the next three chapters I share some of what I have learned from the students I've encountered, analyze common patterns, and offer a few snapshots of individual perspectives. In the process, I draw on interviews with more than 120 students, conducted as part of four different research projects. The three chapters take up themes that consistently emerged from those interviews, and provide the basis for understanding the tensions and misunderstandings that occur inside college classrooms.

CHAPTER 2

THE STUDENT FEAR FACTOR

I WOULD NOT HAVE expected Eva to panic during her first composition class. Eva's reports of her high school preparation for college, her prior experiences in English classes, and her attitude toward writing in general all suggested that she would feel optimistic about Comp 1A. Furthermore, she spoke of her family's strong support for postsecondary education as well as her own commitment to a career that requires a college degree (that of schoolteacher). Eva asserted that although her parents had not put *a lot* of pressure on her (or on her younger sister), they did "make sure we know it's good to come to college." In fact, her parents continually reiterated the school-career connection: "You're working now, but you've got to go to school, because you've got to get a career." Eva's mother served as a role model in this regard: she had recently begun a postsecondary degree program to advance her own career goals. Despite the many reasons for Eva to feel at least relatively confident about her ability to succeed, she felt a sense of alarm when she was introduced to the objectives and structure of her first-semester English class: "That first day, when the professor said that it's going to be an essay after an essay, I was scared. I was like, 'Oh, my God, I'm not going to be able to make it.' . . . Just the fact that she said, 'Oh, you get an essay after an essay after an essay'—that's what scared me."

Eva's case is by no means unique. Regardless of age, ethnicity, academic background, educational goals, or the path to college, students reveal tremendous anxiety about their educational trajectories and ability to succeed in college. This chapter focuses on the "total fear factor," as one student aptly described it—a dimension of the student experience that has emerged in every study I have conducted, across community colleges in different regions of the country and with a highly diverse range of students. The recurrence of this fear factor in such varied contexts attests to its profound effect in shaping students' college experiences. Chapter 2 explores the phenomenon, the nature and source of students' anxiety, and the strategies for managing those fears that students employ.

STUDENT ANXIETY

Regardless of the path that had led each student to college, enrolling in college courses proved to be an immensely stressful transition. For recent high school graduates as well as those outside the "traditional" age range, entering college marked a high-risk and anxiety-provoking transition in their adult lives.

Students fresh from high school, for instance, indicated that the transition into college represented a crucial threshold to adulthood. Melanie, a recent high school graduate and a first-semester college student at Lake Shore Community College in the Southwest, described her initiation to college as follows:

> Here, I've had to really break out of the comfort zone of high school, and I've had to be very much more independent. In high school, if you didn't do homework, you were able to copy off a kid, one of your friends, or you were able to find out information from one of your friends if you skipped a day or whatever. But here, it's pretty much, if I skip, it's my fault. If I don't turn it in, it's my fault. And it's all dependent upon me, and it's made me a lot more independent. It's really pushed me into an area that I don't want to go, but I have to. I mean, it's not, college isn't so much an academic life, but it's also a very social and emotional part of who you are, too.

> In high school, everyone tells you what to do, they tell you what

classes to take, they direct you in certain ways, they put you in categories, and they put you in smart classes or dumb classes. And here in college, nobody does that for you. You have to figure it out on your own. I think college makes you a lot more serious.

Early in her first semester, Melanie had indeed taken a serious approach to college. She had developed both specific long-term career plans and a detailed strategy for realizing them. She would complete two years of college coursework at Lake Shore Community College. At the same time, she would complete some core requirements through the state university's online program. The next step consisted of transferring to the university, where she would earn a B.A. in psychology, then a Ph.D. She knew that an internship would be required for her to become a psychologist, and she had estimated the time it would take for her to become a practicing psychologist. All these steps, she noted, were crucial if she was not to "waste any time," and she described the effort she put into developing a logical plan. "I've had to figure out degree plans, courses at LSCC that can transfer to _____ University, the online courses at State that can transfer to the university; and as much as the counselors have helped me—I mean, they are really good at what they do—but a lot of this is set on you. And I think that really helps you grow as a person, because in the real world, nobody helps you besides your family. Nobody's going to help you. So, yeah, I think I have gotten a little more serious."

In many ways, Melanie fit the profile of a successful college student. She had formulated a clear and seemingly realistic educational plan, she was attending school full-time, she could draw financial and emotional support from her family while pursuing her goals, and she evaded the disadvantages that first-generation college goers face. In addition, she spoke positively about her academic preparation for college; for example, Melanie noted how fortunate she had been to attend a high school where "they didn't pressure us to make great grades, but you were more socially accepted within the school if you were a smart kid." And although Melanie had not necessarily earned the highest grades there—she mentioned "doing a lot better, gradewise" at the community college than she had during high school—she had enjoyed the opportunity to take "higher-level" classes, such as Advanced Placement English Literature. During her final semester in high school, she had taken one class at the community college, which made her feel more prepared for her first semester as a full-time student at the college.

Despite these advantages, Melanie spoke vividly of the fears she confronted on matriculating. Recalling the anxiety she had felt on the first day of the fall semester, she told me, "When I came on my first day here, as I was walking up through that parking lot—I had to park all the way over there at the other end, because it was, like, crazy packed here, on the first day. I remember walking up, thinking, 'I'm all by myself now.' Not literally, but the decisions that I make from today on, I'm going to have to make on my own. My family can advise me, but when it comes down to the nitty-gritty, the decision that I make is going to be my fault, or it's going to be my achievement. You know what I mean? And I think that was just a lot."

This realization, Melanie confided, was too much to handle: "My body just said, 'This is too much stress, this is too much'"— so much that she rushed from the parking lot to the closest women's room, feeling sick to her stomach.

MELANIE

Melanie took four classes her first semester in college: composition, math, psychology, and French. Taking all four at once was challenging, but she felt that she was a serious student, committed to doing well. Throughout our conversation about her classes, Melanie contrasted her college coursework with her high school experience, and in doing so, consistently highlighted the increased academic pressure of college. For example, she described the fast pace of her French class, as compared with the Spanish classes she took in high school: "I never realized how fast college would be—comparing one year of high school with one semester of college. It's really fast pacing. Like, I'm taking French right now, and that has really kicked me in the bum. Because in high school, you have two weeks to learn one section. And here it's like one day you learn a section, the next day you learn another section, it's just so fast paced, but I'm doing pretty good. . . . I think it's just because I've eliminated, like, my close, close friends, and all that kind of stupid high school drama that you go through, because in high school it's not really about academics."

Young adults such as Melanie were not the only ones to view the first semester of college as scary, unfamiliar, or life-changing. Individuals well outside the "traditional" college age range also spoke of the stress of assuming the responsibilities of college. Colleen, who had dropped out of high school at the age of fifteen, decided to return to school when her own children reached school age. At that point, she told herself, "Well, this is the right time for me, and the right time in my life, and I'm mature enough to handle it." Still, she admitted, "it was still really scary. Oh, my God, it was a life-altering change."

Because nearly every student viewed a college degree as essential to her future, they were all embarking on high-stakes ventures. Many lacked the kind of "college knowledge" typical of middle-class students and remained uncertain about how to approach the degree track and their coursework.[1] As a consequence, even as the vast majority of students were convinced that their future success hinged on their obtaining a college degree, they also revealed tremendous anxiety about the educational and occupational paths they were embarking on. A significant component of students' stress was directly linked to their doubts about succeeding in college and realizing their career goals.[2]

For some students, this fear—a natural part of any life transition—was heightened by their past experiences with failure in academic contexts. The frequent mentions of failure in student interviews included tales of having made bad decisions, performed poorly at various levels of elementary and secondary school, failed at specific assignments in high school courses, and failed or dropped classes at the postsecondary level. In addition, many students had fallen down on one or more of the entry-level assessments, whether in reading, writing, or math. In the case of math, the majority of the students I met had failed the test and had been required to enroll in at least one remedial math class before taking courses to fulfill the college math requirement. Thus, for many students, past failure provided objective evidence of their academic inadequacy.

Even students who did not explicitly discuss past failures revealed an underlying lack of confidence, and gnawing doubts about their capacity to succeed in college. For many, their very presence at a community college—the least selective and lowest tier of colleges—offered proof of their minimal academic competence. In other words, whereas admission to a selective college—or even one that is less selective—offers some indication that a student has the capacity to succeed at that school, even this tenuous assurance is not available to students who enter a college with an open-admissions policy.

THE FEAR FACTOR

By enrolling in college courses, committing to a degree plan, and envisioning long-term objectives that depended on success at the community college, each student had stepped into the role of college student. The many students who seriously doubted their ability to succeed, however, were anxiously waiting for their shortcomings to be exposed, at which point they would be stopped from pursuing their goals. Fragile and fearful, these students expressed their concern in several ways: in reference to college professors, particular courses or subject matter, and the entire notion of college itself—whether at the two- or the four-year level. At the core of different expressions of fear, however, were the same feelings of dread and the apprehension that success in college would prove to be an unrealizable dream.[3]

Students admitted to feeling intimidated by professors' academic knowledge and by teachers' power to assess students and assign grades. Essentially, students were afraid that the professor would irrevocably confirm their academic inadequacy. When students described their stereotypical image of the university professor, a coherent picture emerged. Associating this ideal professor type with prestigious universities, students portrayed professors as "looking down on" students. One student, for example, spoke of his preconceived image of college professors as "all high and mighty," and Colleen spoke of the "pompous-ass professor" type. She associated this type with the elite universities, noting, "When you think of Yale, you're thinking pompous-ass professors."

From Colleen's perspective, her philosophy instructor tended "to act like he's teaching at Yale or something." During her interview with me, she addressed him in absentia, with this request: "Come down to our level a little bit. I know you have a lot of stuff to teach us, but don't be so high on that pedestal that we can't reach you." Her belief in the philosophy professor's clear superiority shaped Colleen's approach to the course. She explained,

> It got to where I did not feel comfortable approaching him about anything, because I felt like he was this so-smart guy that I'm going to look really stupid in his eyes if I ask him any questions at all. And so I don't feel comfortable asking him anything. I just go to class, and I sit in the back of the classroom now, whereas I started at the front of the classroom. I sit in the back, behind whoever else I can find, so he doesn't even have to look at me. So I'm just kind of hiding in the back, thinking, "Yes, I'm going to pass this class, somehow."

Colleen's philosophy teacher was not at all typical. Except for Colleen, when students alluded to the "so-smart" or "high and mighty professors," they noted that their community college professors did not fall into that category. Melanie, for instance, insisted that her community college instructors did not match her preconceptions about college professors. "When I was a high school student, I very much got the idea that college was very anonymous, that all you were, really, was a name on a page. You know, you really weren't a person." The difference between the stereotypical professor and students' actual professors did not mean, however, that students were unafraid of or unintimidated by their community college instructors.

Both Serena and Ryan provided examples of professors who were not "all high and mighty," but rather "kind of friendly." Yet their interactions with these professors still reflected an intimidating distance between professor and student. In describing his history professor, for instance, Ryan noted, "There's kind of something about him that, I don't know, makes me kind of hesitant to say something to him. He's kind of friendly, but it's just, I don't really know, something about him is just . . ." (his voice trailed off). Serena offered a similar description of her hesitancy about meeting professors during their office hours. "Like, some professors will be like, 'Oh, I'll be in my office,' but you're real hesitant to go to them, because of the way they are."

In fact, Colleen's avoidance strategy in her philosophy course represented a frequent student behavior. In this case, her approach was particularly interesting because she had demonstrated a high level of assertiveness in other situations—both on her own behalf and for other students. She had confronted the tutors at the writing center, for example, and had advised several younger students in her classes to consult with their instructors when problems arose. That Colleen would resort to hiding from her philosophy teacher suggests that other younger or less assertive students would be even more likely to react that way to stressful classroom encounters.

A wide range of courses, subject matter, and assignments caused students to worry. Math and composition, however, evoked by far the greatest anxiety for the vast majority of students. Students' fear of the composition course was particularly intense.[4] As the portal to more exclusive classes, composition plays a crucial role in selection of students. Those who successfully complete the course are judged proficient in the general writing skills deemed necessary for further academic study. Thus, the outcome for each student in composition holds important consequences for his or her educational trajectory and ability to succeed as a college student. Not by coincidence, among community college offerings this high-stakes course has some of the highest dropout rates—second only to those in math courses.

Kyra, who put off taking the course until her very last semester, noted, "I just had a fear of English, like this total fear factor." Likewise, Linda, who enrolled in and then dropped the course multiple times before finally completing it, explained, "The only reason why I waited is because I hate writing. I was always afraid of it—I think I've always had that problem."

Students' explanations for their anxiety often highlighted inadequate instruction in the past. "Oh, high school teachers [sigh]. I wrote two papers, I think, and that was it. And we never had to edit or anything. Yeah, I knew I was going to have a very hard time" (Suzanne).

Significantly, however, students who feared composition class did not necessarily perceive their high school preparation as inadequate. Anxiety and low self-confidence also plagued students who spoke favorably of their former English teachers or commented on the rigor of their high school English curriculum.[5]

This was certainly true for Eva, the student we met at the beginning of this chapter whose first day of class caused her to think, "I'm not going to make it." Jenn—another student who had earned As in her high school English classes—offered a more vivid description of her first day of college, at which point she, too, questioned whether she could handle the work required in composition. "I just saw all the work, and my heart was beating, and I'm just thinking, 'This is not real. There's no way college can be this hard.' It was just like they were throwing information at you, and just expecting you to be okay with it."

Although male students were much less likely than female students to offer unsolicited accounts of feeling anxious or unprepared, they too admitted that particular courses had generated nervousness. Diego, for example, expressed a sense of amazement at his success in composition class, particularly in light of his dislike of writing. As he explained, "I like reading, but I don't like writing. So I was surprised at my accomplishments in this class."

> *Becky:* So it kind of sounds like you were very nervous about how well you would do.
>
> *Diego:* Yes, yes, yes. I did come in like that. This is my worst, my— actually, I'm passing this class—but this was the one I was most afraid of.

Similarly, Carlos was worried about submitting essays in composition class "because of the fear and because I didn't know exactly what [the teacher] wanted."

Looking back, Carlos explained how his fears had initially paralyzed him, making his coursework more difficult: "It was like I thought I wouldn't make it, like I wasn't going to be able to make it. And I made it hard and it wasn't that hard." When I asked how he made his coursework harder, he elaborated, "It was the negative touch. It wasn't that I couldn't make it or I didn't do this right or I did this wrong. It was just that I was afraid. . . . Maybe it was the fear of college, too. . . . I think that's one of the things that makes a lot of people fail."

When asked, near the end of the semester, about their experiences at the start of the semester, some students admitted nonchalantly that they had anticipated that their courses would be more difficult. Claudia for instance commented, "I just expected more work. Like I'd never have time for anything else." Such students did not explicitly mention any anxiety around their original expectations, but it is possible that they, too, had experienced some nervousness at the start of their community college experience.

Students who expressed confidence in their ability to succeed at the community college level were not necessarily as certain about the four-year level. Several students noted that taking classes at the community college had made them change their minds about transferring to a four-year college. Taking courses had convinced Nereida, for example, that she wasn't really "college material." She planned to continue at the two-year college but had decided not to transfer. Similarly, Susan did not want to transfer to the nearby university, she explained, "'cause I don't think I can hang." In reference to his own plan to transfer to a four-year college in California, Sebastian mused: "I just wonder how I would do at a four-year college, like at a Cal State or a UC. I'm sure things are turned up a notch over there."

His experience at Hillcrest Community College (HCC) had led Sebastian to conclude that you can "use HCC to mold your education; then, if you're really serious, you can go on to a four-year college." Describing himself as not yet motivated "all the way," Sebastian contended that once he reached that point, he would "probably really cut back on work and just focus on school and try to give a good push for a year or two, get something accomplished." His fear revolved around the four-year experience in store for him once he did get really serious. "I'm just hoping that these classes that I'm taking aren't these totally, like—I don't know the word—more like a waste of time; like doing all this easy stuff, when really I'm not aware of all the higher classes that I should be trying to take and get into." Nikki also confessed to her past and present fears of college. While discussing her transfer goals, she concluded: "So, we shall see. It's scary—very scary. . . . I'm so unsure of what to expect at the next level. It was scary to come here—I wasn't sure what to expect, but it was okay. It turned out okay, I guess."

SEBASTIAN

This was Sebastian's second semester at the college, and he was taking three classes while working part-time at a video store. The previous semester, he had worked full-time and started with four courses, but he found that he "started to fall behind." Since he had changed his work schedule, Sebastian wasn't particularly worried about his courses. "Like English: so far it's good, it's pretty easy, not really bad at all, compared to high school—I hated English." In part he attributed it to his own maturity as a student: "Now that I'm in college, I'm a little more mature and . . . I can get something out of it now."

Sebastian hadn't yet enrolled in any college-level classes, however; that semester, he was taking three basic skills classes, one for math, one for reading, and one for writing. In all the classes, but especially the English courses, he felt confident about his ability to do well. "I feel prepared; I feel comfortable doing all the work. It's all easy for me." Sebastian's anxiety was reserved for the future courses; he admitted, "But, um, I'm going to see how English 1A goes, because that's like freshman English."

FEAR MANAGEMENT

Fear of failing as college students drove some to employ preventive strategies. Choosing such actions (or inaction), however, could easily divert students from accomplishing their original goals. This risk was what puzzled me about students like Eva. When I interviewed her, she and her classmates in Composition 1A were nearly all assured of passing the course. Yet even she, a competent and conscientious student who "always knew [she] would attend college," had considered quitting on day one of the course. Nor was she the only one to respond in that way. Jenn's anxieties on her first day almost led her to drop out of college altogether. Jenn prefaced her account by saying, "I really wasn't ready to come, at all. I wasn't ready for it altogether, just wasn't ready for another year of school. I was in a new town, at a new school. And I just didn't know what to expect."

The first day of school was a Tuesday, a day when all her courses were scheduled to meet. Before going to the first class of the day, Jenn spoke to her mother.

I called her up, and I said, "I'm on my way to school." She says, "Okay, I'll talk to you later on," and I said "okay." I went to my first class, had like a four-and-a-half-hour break, and then went to my other three, went home, and I thought, "I quit."

Then I called my mom up, and I tell her, "I quit. Yeah, I quit here." She asks, "How do you plan on living?" and I say, "I don't know. I don't know how I plan on living. I don't care." She says, "Jenn, it can't be that bad," and I say, "You want to hear what the hell I have to do?" And I went syllabus by syllabus, day by day. And she was just like, "Well, just take it one day at a time. Don't get overwhelmed." And I'm just thinking, "Don't get overwhelmed? It's a little late for that!"

So I sat there and bawled with Mama for three hours. Then I talked to my sister, and my sister tells me, "I'll help you out." So eventually, after like four hours of talking with my mom, and an hour and a half talking with my sister, they convinced me that I could do this, that I've been through tougher stuff than this, and that it'd be no big deal.

Clearly, quitting is the ultimate fear management strategy, because it offers a means of eliminating the source of anxiety; however, students did not necessarily opt out of school altogether. Other strategies offered students ways of continuing their studies, while warding off the worst forms of personal failure.

JENN

Although Jenn had received all As in high school, she described herself as "absolutely not" prepared for college. When I asked her to explain, she told me that her older sister, who had taken Advanced Placement (AP) courses in high school, had reported being totally unprepared for college. In fact, her sister was constantly challenging Jenn, telling her, "'You need to take harder classes—these are just simple classes.'" Her sister also told Jenn, "'You're making all As. There is a problem here.' And she's like, 'You don't study. You barely do your homework.' She said, 'You know, you wait until the last minute to do your homework.' And she's like, 'I just don't see how you're making all As, when you're really not doing anything.'" Jenn was so ner-

vous about college that for the entire summer after high school graduation she tried to avoid thinking about registering for classes at the
community college she planned to attend. If her mother hadn't been
"getting on her" about it, she might not have followed through. Describing how the pressure affected her, Jenn provided an example
from the summer: "So my mom was just on me. 'We need to get your
scheduling done, dah, dah, dah,' and it was like, 'I'm overwhelmed.
Don't bother me, don't talk to me.' I didn't talk to her for like three
weeks."

One such strategy consisted of scaling back. Several students
had been admitted to nearby four-year colleges, but had chosen
instead to start their college careers in a less stressful environment. Adriana told me, that she had made a good decision, stating, "I think it's a good way to start because I'm afraid if I would
have gone straight to [Research University], I would have been
stressed out, because it would have been such a bigger thing."

Similarly, Ashley told me, "I'm just kind of getting my feet wet
in the whole college experience thing. I'm new to the city, so I'm
new to the area and everything, and I got accepted to Western
State, but I got—I don't want to say I got scared, but I just
wanted to save my own money, not be a burden on my parents.
So I'm doing that and going to school here, and it is [pause]—it's
smaller classes, and you get to [pause]—it's better. I'm gradually
getting up there. And then I'll go, I'm going to go to Western
State probably next fall, or the fall after—I'm not sure." When I
asked her if she could break it down and assign percentages to
her different reasons, Ashley came up with an estimate of 20 percent for saving money. "I really don't want to be a burden, and
I'm probably going to get like financial aid and stuff. But, yeah,
it's not that big. . . . I don't know, maybe like 20 percent." As far
as the time to "gradually get up there" and be ready for the four-
year college, "probably over 50 percent. Yeah, that's probably
the biggest reason, is just really wanting to be ready."

For Ashley, the underlying fear involved being exposed—in

front of the teacher and her peers—as too stupid for college classes. "I don't want to be the stupid kid in class, where everyone else is raising their hand, and I'm the only one not. And I know it's not going to be like that, but it's one of my biggest fears."

In both instances, highly capable students with excellent records of performance in high school took themselves out of high-risk situations by scaling down and starting at LSCC.

Students with more marginal academic backgrounds were similarly driven by their fears to scale back their educational goals. Nereida and Susan were taking themselves off the baccalaureate track. Others spoke of newly formulated career plans, born of a desire to do "less school." Examples of students who spoke of such scaled-back plans included Suzanne, who was considering cosmetology, and Mariella, who spoke of earning a certificate instead of an associate's degree. For still others, scaling back would result in their withdrawing from school altogether.

A second fear management strategy was to redefine success and failure. Some students, who described the advantages that sprang from specific experiences of failure, exhibited remarkable resilience in the face of disappointments and derailed plans. This ability to reframe disappointments and failures as fortuitous twists of fate was expressed most eloquently by a Latino student named Carlos. Midway through his first semester of college, Carlos's composition instructor, Michelle, recommended that he withdraw from the course, to avoid receiving an F.[6] When I asked Carlos how disappointed he was that he would have to repeat the course, he responded with the phrase "No hay mal que por bien no venga" (There is no bad thing that can't turn out for the good) and explained, "It's okay, because now I'm going to focus more on the other classes. And right now, music is really hard stuff right now, so I'm going to focus on music and my other classes. It won't affect me on my financial aid because I had fifteen hours, so now I have twelve."

Other students seemed to be formulating protective rationalizations for imminent failure. For instance, near the end of the semester, Yolanda disclosed that she had many outstanding composition assignments. She had attended every class session, and noted that she had learned a lot of grammar (especially pronouns) by taking the class. In the same conversation, she offered a range of definitions of success in Comp 1A:

> Success for one person can be, "I've actually conquered it by making the A I wanted to make." "I went to all the classes," can be a success. "I flunked the classes, but yet I understand what a pronoun is," can be a success. . . .
>
> And so you win some, you lose some. I may lose three hundred dollars and flunk in this class, but when I take the class again, I guarantee you that I'll come back with a little bit more fire under me and say, "Okay, I know what you want done. So I know what I need, and I'm going to get it done."

With this revised definition of success, Yolanda could finish the semester without completing the assignments and therefore fail the course, yet still retain a sense of efficacy that would enable her to return to LSCC the following semester to retake Comp 1A. In fact, Yolanda did not pass Comp 1A that semester. During the interview, she had expressed confidence that she was able to do the required coursework, and yet, two-thirds of the way through the semester, she had not yet submitted any of the essay assignments to her instructor. Yolanda was not unique in this regard. Across six sections of composition at LSCC, I observed students who attended class through the end of the semester, completed the assigned readings, and participated in the in-class activities—yet failed to submit written work for their instructors to grade. Still other students had disappeared altogether, silently withdrawing from the course and joining the 40 percent who did not complete Comp 1A.

A third fear management strategy consisted simply of avoiding any formal assessment. Every assessment-related activity posed the risk of exposing to others (both professors and peers) what students already suspected: their overall unfitness for college. Thus, not participating in classroom discussions, avoiding conversations with the professor—whether inside or outside the classroom—or choosing not to attend class sessions offered fear-driven students another reprieve from exposure. Students have admitted that silence during class—whether in whole-group or small-group configurations—results from anxiety, not from laziness or lack of caring. Some students deal with test-taking anxiety by avoiding particular tests; others end up taking the test, only to stop attending class before they find out the results. The greatest risk, of course, lies in graded assessments of student performance. In the absence of evidence from assessments, students can still cling—however tenuously—to their identity as college students.

Jenn, who had reported feeling overwhelmed on day one by the coursework outlined on various syllabi, decided not to quit immediately, but she came to that decision only after hours of discussion with her family. When I asked Jenn how often, after that first day at LSCC, she reconsidered dropping out, she replied, "I would think that, probably, with every first test that there was." In other words, the prospect of submitting the first graded assignment for each course was the most terrifying part of the semester. Barbara told about her first English class, during which the instructor administered an in-class writing assignment. With a sense of hopelessness, Barbara attempted to draft some sort of response; and at the end of the class, Barbara recalled, "I walked up to [the professor's] desk. I handed her my paper and I said, 'I don't know what you want written down. I have no idea what an essay is.' . . . She looked at me and I told her, 'I'm not coming back.'" This particular example highlights the irony of such avoidance strategies, that students' efforts to manage their fear of failure can easily lead to failure.

Elisa's experience with the research paper assignment illustrates the extent to which her fear of failure drove her to the brink of actual failure. On the day the research paper was due in Julie's class, I had a conversation with Elisa and Charmaine, neither of whom was ready to submit a draft of the assignment. Whereas Charmaine expressed confidence that she would submit one soon, Elisa spoke of her loathing for the research paper assignment. In fact, she told us, she had withdrawn from Comp 1A during the spring semester after getting stuck on this very assignment. At this point in the fall course, with Julie as her instructor, Elisa had chosen a topic (the influence of media images on women) and begun brainstorming about possible theses; however, she voiced concern about finding more sources and demonstrated hesitance regarding the appropriateness of the topic for the research paper assignment. When I asked whether she had talked to her instructor, Julie, about those concerns, she replied, "But I feel so bad—I'm so far behind and I don't want her to know." Instead, Elisa thought that she would probably withdraw from the course and try again next semester.

Upon urging from Charmaine and me, Elisa did meet with Julie to discuss the research paper. Julie later reported to me that Elisa had successfully completed the assignment. "Her research paper she finally submitted to me was A work. I mean, I chuckled. I wrote a comment back to her: 'LOL—I'm laughing out loud because your paper is awesome, and you were worried sick about submitting this paper to me, and this is your best paper.'"

When it came to learning, Elisa's strategy of avoidance was clearly counterproductive. Such an approach to the assignment made sense only in light of her conviction that she was not a competent college student. From this perspective, error—whether past or potential, real or imagined—plays a destructive role, by chipping away at each student's self-conception as a competent college student. Not surprisingly, students exhibited very low tolerance for feeling confused or making mistakes, phenomena they could easily attribute to their own inadequacy rather than to the process of learning new skills or information.[7]

This was certainly true of Natalie, a second-semester student at a California college. During her interview, Natalie assessed herself as entirely "unready" for college, attributing it to a personal character flaw—a form of fear-induced lack of effort.

> I'm scared of hard stuff. I'm intimidated by hard stuff, so that's probably holding me back. I need more courage. . . . I'm a scaredy-cat; I say, "That class is too hard," instead of trying it out and applying myself. That's what's wrong with me.
>
> I turned in my first paper and I got an X. I mean, you're supposed to get like, a B over X, or a C over X, so that you can have a chance to fix what you made a mistake in and then get that C. And I didn't get anything over that X—I just got an X. . . . See, that's why I don't turn anything in. . . . That's why I don't like turning anything in, because every time I do, I get a bad grade.

Natalie had carefully examined the syllabus for some clue about the mysterious X she'd received but still did not understand what it meant. Her friend, also in the class, chimed in, "That just means you got to rewrite the whole thing." Natalie disagreed, however. According to the written policies, "He said no rewriting. He said, Don't rewrite the papers, just correct them."

It is difficult to understand why Natalie did not complete any assignments after her initial X grades. Not only did she demonstrate familiarity with the syllabus and various course documents, in noting the correct instructions for students who receive an "over X" grade, but her understanding of the regulations also reflected careful reading of these relatively complicated texts. Yet her confusion about the X stymied her, instead of propelling her to investigate further. She continued to attend class, she participated in the small-group exercises, and she prepared for in-class quizzes. She did nothing about the incomplete essay, however. Nor did she submit any other essays. Instead, she avoided the problem. While her instructor waited fruitlessly for Natalie to seek his help, he assumed that she did not care about the course.

In the end, both teacher and student interpreted her performance as the result of individual deficits.

IMPLICATIONS FOR STUDENT SUCCESS

Using the example of his first math test of the semester, Carlos discussed his realization that the best plan was to work through the fear. On the day of the math test, he related, "I got panicked. And then I thought, 'Well, I'm going to try it,' and then I started writing and it was okay. That was it. I just got two problems wrong. And actually I got the first- or the second-highest grade in the class."

Carlos thus pinpointed the conundrum facing fearful students: fear drives them to the point of quitting, yet making the effort in the face of that fear may provide the evidence that they can succeed.

Of huge significance regarding this phenomenon is the fact that I generally interviewed students at the end of the semester. By that point, many others had already quietly disappeared from the class. A few of the students who attended the last few weeks of class might have ended up failing the course, but for the most part, I interviewed the most successful students. At the same time, I do not believe that I would have gained the same insights about student fear had I interviewed students who did not persist. Nor do I believe that the students I interviewed at the end of the semester would have admitted their prior fears had they not believed that they were going to complete their courses successfully. In other words, students who acknowledged their fears did so in the past tense; they had felt that way at the start of the semester but had progressed over the course of it toward feeling less afraid and more confident. I suspect that had they still harbored those shameful feelings of inadequacy, the instinct to avoid being evaluated would have prevented them from admitting their fears, perhaps even to themselves.

The depth of fear among the most successful and resilient students—students who had persisted in their courses until the end of the semester—suggests that at least some students who had withdrawn from the course or failed to complete the graded coursework were pushed over the brink by their fears, into failure. For individuals who started the semester feeling unequal to "college student" demands, it was easy to perceive every dimension of college and college coursework as overly confusing and too difficult. Such students avoided the forms of active engagement that would have improved their chances of succeeding, while simultaneously diverting instructors' attention from the core reason for their counterproductive behavior. In other words, such defenses against fear seriously undermined their chances of passing the course. In light of the large number of students who fail or withdraw from Comp 1A at community colleges, it is very likely that many employed the counterproductive strategies described by the students I have spoken with. Students like Jenn and Eva felt like quitting at the start of the semester, but other students actually did so at various points throughout the semester.

With a few exceptions, the composition students I interviewed had mustered enough courage to submit written work throughout the semester and ultimately completed the course successfully. Judged by the end-of-semester outcomes, the depth of fear that the interview respondents had experienced at the start of the semester was unwarranted. Once students overcame the biggest obstacle—once they submitted the most fear-inducing assignment—their performance far exceeded their initial pessimistic predictions. They had been able to overcome their fears without resorting to passive strategies of disengagement or dropping out.

For those who did pass the course, one of the most important lessons was that when they submitted the writing assignments, their deepest fears were disproved. For Kyra, who spoke to me of her "total fear factor" in Comp 1A, doing well in the class provided evidence of her writing competence. As she put it, "So that kind of in itself indicates that I'm not as bad as I thought I was. And my fear is maybe just in my head, rather than actual fact." Similarly, Linda concluded at the end of the semester, "I hated writing, but now I feel that I know that I can. I feel better now. I'm not afraid like I was before."

Similarly, Jenn, who had left the first class session ready to quit school, described how her attitude changed after she had submitted the first graded assignment. "But once I got my first paper accepted for English, I was so excited. It made me want to go and write some more. Yeah, it made me want to go and write some more, and after my second paper, my mom just told me, 'I don't think anybody's given you the chance to write. I don't think anybody's given you what you needed, to learn.'"

Individuals who are familiar with what is required and who are relatively confident from the start of their success as college students are most likely to achieve success. Conversely, those who are least conversant with the norms of higher education are at a distinct disadvantage; they are more likely to feel like outsiders and to doubt their ability to fit in. Indeed, for fearful students, every interaction in the classroom and with their professors outside class holds the potential to confirm their feelings of inadequacy. Yet the same strategies that relieve their fear can prove counterproductive for completing college coursework. In particular, avoiding assessment precludes the chance of proving their academic merit. Thus the fear of failure—rather than actual failure or evidence of unsuitability—prevents full commitment and engagement. How such fears and counterproductive strategies might be countered is therefore an important consideration in promoting student success. How individual professors have addressed the issue—indeed, *that* professors need to address the issue—lies at the heart of Chapter 6.

CHAPTER 3

STUDENT ASPIRATIONS

GETTING THE BIGGEST BANG FOR THE BUCK

THE STUDENT FEAR FACTOR outlined in Chapter 2 presents a puzzle. In the case of students who begin college believing they are likely or certain to fail, what motivates them to pursue higher education at all? When self-doubts and anxiety about succeeding in college result in disengagement strategies, what prevents more students from quitting school altogether? In other words, rather than ask why and how so many college students meet with failure, perhaps it is more useful to consider how students persist in the face of such powerful urges to quit.

The answer to this puzzle lies in students' motivations for attending college. Consistently, students explained their participation in higher education as a means to earn a decent living and reach financial stability. As Nikki declared, "You gotta be ready for college," in order to face the high-stakes venture; and for the vast majority of students, being "ready" involved commitment to "being something" or "getting somewhere in life." Getting somewhere in life is predicated on achieving specific career and financial goals, and this occupational motive can prove strong enough to supersede students' academic self-doubts or prior history of disengagement with school.

This distinctly economic purpose for going to college—to acquire credentials to advance career goals—is significant because it shapes students' college experience in several crucial ways. It defines college as something to invest in, something people must buy, in the expectation that it will be useful in their career endeavors. Viewing college as necessary to long-term career aspirations and a secure financial future motivates students to seek the most useful and efficient educational path, the one that will help them accomplish their career goals most directly.

This chapter details the results of students' instrumental approach to higher education. Beginning with an overview of students' primary educational objectives, I discuss students' definition of the benefits of college along with the short-term costs and potential pitfalls. I then turn to students' strategies for minimizing the costs, exploring how pursuit of a useful education affects the decisions students make about when to attend college and what degree program to work toward, as well as their views on whether the experience has proved worthwhile.

OCCUPATIONAL GOALS

Despite the differences in age, educational trajectory, work history, and degree plans, college students consistently explain their attendance as the means of improving their occupational prospects: the way to become a "professional," to "make a decent living," to "get somewhere." As Susan put it, "I need to *be* something." In fact, Susan expressed an urgency about "being something" that other students didn't necessarily voice. In Susan's case, progress through college had been delayed by academic and personal considerations. Her entry-level English and math skills were low enough that she was required to take several basic skills courses, so after three years of college, she was still not ready for college-level math or English courses. Even so, she had taken "quite a few" psychology classes and found the subject to be "plain" and "too boring." This had led her to reconsider her plan to become a psychologist. In the meantime, she had experienced "a lot of drama" with an ex-boyfriend, and that had prevented her from thinking through her options for the future.

Consequently, she told me, "I still don't know what I want to be or what I like to do, and I haven't really sat down to think about it. . . . I mean, I'm just twenty-one, but it just seems like I'm this ancient person that's desperate for an end, or some sort of goal. . . . I just want to be something already."

Among the students I have formally interviewed, only two explained their attendance in terms other than career goals. These two students were Ruth, a retired accountant, who was taking English courses for pleasure, and Natalie, a recent high school graduate. Natalie was not sure about her educational or occupational objectives, and explained her presence at the community college by saying: "My mom said, 'You need to go to school or something, cause you ain't gonna be here [at home] all day,' so I came here."

Certainly, students' career goals encompassed a wide range of occupations, and their educational or occupational plans varied considerably in their degree of specificity. Some students had targeted specific jobs (such as elementary school teacher, police officer, or paralegal), others were pursuing particular fields of study (computer science, psychology, "something in engineering"), and still others were exploring the possible options as they engaged in coursework.

The majority of students viewed a subbaccalaureate degree or certification as the first stage on a longer educational path. Some students imagined persisting through a continuous stretch of schooling to their baccalaureate degree. Others envisioned earning a two-year degree, then stopping out and resuming college coursework after a stint in the full-time workforce. The vast majority explicitly mentioned a four-year degree as central to their long-term goals, and some aspired to graduate-level degrees in law, psychology, and medicine.

Students, whether they were aiming for specific jobs or entertained vague concepts about possible career paths, invariably highlighted the dual economic and occupational benefits of a college degree. Kevin, who had graduated from high school the previous spring, noted, "I want to get a degree in computer networking or whatever it's called. Well, I want to get my Cisco certification, then get an internship while I'm getting my Cisco certification, and then I could get a job and then get paid once I get my CCNA [Cisco Certified Network Administration]. And then, I guess, get a degree, like a bachelor's or something like that, and then get paid even more."

Kevin connected each step of his education—community college coursework, Cisco certification, and bachelor's degree—to corresponding phases in his employment trajectory, meanwhile indicating that the aim of obtaining a bachelor's degree is to "get paid even more."

Sebastian defined the purpose of college in the same way, although he had not yet mapped out a specific career path (as Kevin had). According to Sebastian's account, the occupational benefits of college represented commonly accepted wisdom "everyone" possessed. "Right now I'm just going with what everyone thinks you should do when you get out of high school nowadays—I mean, you need to go to college; a high school diploma isn't going to get you the salary-paying job you need to support yourself."

SEBASTIAN

Although Sebastian wasn't sure what kind of career he wanted to pursue, he knew that he didn't want to continue doing jobs that are available to high school graduates. Of his current job, he complained, "I've been there for like a year, and I just got a raise, and it was only fifteen cents. But that's why I'm going to school, so I can get out of there."

Sebastian did have some ideas about what he didn't want to do. He knew that construction was one of his current options, but "I just wouldn't want to do manual labor, or even try to work at the minimum wage, and do that forty hours a week. I'd rather try to get something I enjoy, something at a little higher level. I don't know, though; I'm still exploring my options."

Therefore, unlike students who had more specific career plans, Sebastian wasn't entirely sure how he would proceed in college, noting, "I'm not sure I know what I want to major in, or anything like that. My plan is just take up all these general ed. courses and move towards something that strikes me as interesting. I'm hoping I'll come across a certain class or something that I'll want to delve deeper into. Or something that I'm good at, like, I get a good grade in."

Students cited a good many sources on the wisdom of earning a college degree, including parents, peers, and mentors. Older students attributed their recognition to their own experiences in the workplace. This hard-earned knowledge proved more persuasive than any other source. Despite pressure from his parents to attend college, for example, Miguel was not convinced of the value of college until he had spent time looking for full-time work. After graduating from high school, Miguel had planned not to attend college. He joined the military, "did his three years" of service, then moved into the civilian workforce. Only then did he reconsider the value of college. When I asked him why he had changed his mind about attending college, he replied, "Because I worked already. There's nothing out there. Well, there are jobs, but they're menial. They don't pay anything. And education: you get a chance for good opportunities."[1] This experience had propelled Miguel, at the age of twenty-four, to consider college seriously for the first time. He formulated a plan to complete two years of coursework at the community college, then transfer to a four-year college to complete a B.A. in sociology.

Hugh came to a similar realization after taking a break from school. "I've just—my parents have always influenced me towards it [college]. But the main thing was working—I've always worked for eighteen dollars an hour or so, so I've never had a good job, and I want to get started on a career one of these days."

Although Hugh's parents had influenced him to go to college, "the main thing" that propelled him to enroll was his work experience, most recently his job on a construction crew. Unless he earned a postsecondary degree, he contended, he would be limited to lower-paying jobs and would remain unqualified for the kind of work that constitutes a real career. Hugh entered the community college with very specific degree plans: he intended to earn LVN certification at the two-year level, then continue for an R.N. degree. For Hugh, this represented a clear path towards a real career.

In sum, these college students all agreed: the primary benefit of higher education is the improved occupational prospects that reward a postsecondary credential. In describing their career aspirations, students viewed higher education as a requirement for their occupational and financial goals. Even so, the decision to attend college was complicated by the need to balance the eventual benefits of a postsecondary degree with the short-term costs and the potential pitfalls.

SHORT-TERM COSTS

For students of every age, school and work were in tension. Although a degree could improve work prospects, college attendance was accompanied by work-related opportunity costs. Kyra, a twenty-five-year-old student in graphic design, explained the fundamental tension by stating, "I'm getting older, and as you get older, you need to kind of have more security. You want to be in the workforce quick."

Students spoke of two kinds of costs. The price of attendance (tuition and books), compounded by lost income, constituted the first. For most students, even part-time college attendance limited employment options; therefore, taking postsecondary courses decreased their short-term income. Because of these financial considerations, the time students could devote to pursuing further education was limited in duration. The second cost came from interrupted advancement in the employment students would have been pursuing if they were not enrolled in college. Therefore, participation in higher education involved a gamble: they had to risk losing more certain advancement in favor of potentially greater (but less certain) increases in future income.

Student's decisions about college often reflected this tension between short-term and long-term considerations. For instance, once Miguel decided that college was the necessary next step to improve his economic prospects, he did not matriculate immediately. Instead, he waited until he had made all his car payments, then enrolled. "So no car payment to worry about. It's all financial. It's all a financial issue." Once this immediate financial issue was resolved, Miguel committed to pursuing a baccalaureate in sociology.

Yolanda was also a student who delayed matriculation. She had decided to take a full-time job right out of high school, in part to get a sense of workplace expectations. After working for a few years, she would "go to college, then come back with a degree and apply it all together." After one year of full-time employment, however, Yolanda was ready to return to school. "And so then after my hard knocks throughout the year, I'm like, 'I need an education.'"

In explaining her path to college, Yolanda voiced no regret about taking the break between high school and college. To the contrary, when she considered what might have happened had she started college immediately after graduating from high school, she described the worst case imaginable as her finding herself with a degree in hand but no job prospects. She thus considered her decision to delay higher education in favor of full-time work as well justified. "If I had started [college] right when I got out [of high school], I would be almost two years in college right now. And I would be even more depressed if I'm in college for two years and I still can't get a state job or I still can't get this or that job." Unlike students such as Miguel or Hugh, who were several years older and had more work experience, Yolanda did not return to school with a specified educational or career goal. Instead, she was driven simply by the conviction that some sort of postsecondary credential was necessary. "I ain't sure if I want to be an EMT, nurse, lawyer—just whatever pays, so I can get out of debt. That's my goal."

In the meantime, Yolanda was attending college full-time and working part-time for hourly pay. In addition, she had moved back in with her parents to minimize the financial stress. These measures, she reasoned, would suffice to afford her a short stint in college, but she needed to start earning substantially more money in the near future.

Although working part-time enabled Yolanda to attend school full-time, her job presented several dilemmas over the course of the semester. Financially, Yolanda needed the work. Consequently, in time conflicts between school and work, work took priority. By the end of the semester, when work demands increased (for the holiday season), Yolanda was required to work overtime and was assigned hours that competed with her coursework.

Such examples show how students' primary motivation for going to college—the desire for a good career and financial security—often collides with their immediate financial and job-related circumstances. Not surprisingly, this tension between short-term and long-term considerations not only shapes students' choices about whether and when to attend college, but also affects decisions about how long to attend, what kind of degree to obtain, and how to earn that degree most efficiently.

Charmaine, a thirty-three-year-old African American woman, was completing her final semester of credits for the degree of Associate in Applied Science (AAS). Charmaine's approach to college amply illustrates how her decisions were driven by the need to make sure she approached her college experience as efficiently as possible and derived the greatest possible benefit from it. She accounted for her presence at the community college by declaring, "I had never had any school. I had experience. I was pretty much maxed out to where I could go, as far as promotions and financial reasoning. So I felt like I had to start school, because I needed to get some type of education in my background. And that's what made me start going part-time. I was trying to get an education, because education is really important right now. That's pretty much what employers are looking for: people who have education."

Charmaine had worked full-time since graduating from high school, so her understanding of employer expectations was rooted in personal experience. Her work experience had increased Charmaine's interest in earning a college degree and had led her to enroll in college courses on a part-time basis several years earlier. Being "downsized" from her job had increased her sense of urgency about earning a degree. Only by taking advantage of a job retraining grant, Charmaine contended, was she able to afford to attend school full-time. Indeed, over the past two years, before receiving the grant funds, she had been enrolling in one course per semester.

Accordingly, Charmaine's priority was to use her time and money efficiently. With her limited financial resources, she pointed out, she needed to move back into full-time employment as quickly as possible. In her view, the most efficient approach to her full-time stint at the community college was to fulfill the minimum requirements for her associate's degree. "Right now I'm just mainly taking the required courses for my degree plan." She added, "A lot of people are . . . saying, 'Okay, I'm going to transfer to a four-year college,' and they're taking courses outside their degree plan. If you have financial backing, that's good, but if you don't have that money behind you right now, I feel like it's best to go for the ones that are most important right now, and then pay. Who knows? Maybe I'll get a job and they'll pay for it, and I can afford to go, take all this other stuff that I will need to transfer into a four-year, but right now I need to go for the associate's classes."

In order to reach her long-term educational goal, a bachelor's in engineering, she planned to return to the community college at a later time to earn the remaining transfer credits. She hoped that her next employer would finance further education, so that she could return to college with "the financial backing." For the immediate future, though, she was focusing on the subbaccalaureate degree in electronics. "I want to at least get the associate, so if something happens . . . at least I will have the associate's degree. I'll have something."

In this context, Charmaine believed not that spending time or money on transfer courses would be a bad idea, but rather that she could simply not afford to be unemployed for any longer than absolutely necessary. For her, the key to managing the costs of college lay in carefully choosing degree plans and course schedules.

Marshaling scarce resources—particularly time and money—is only part of what is needed to participate in higher education. Students' occupational and financial goals have to be powerful enough to overcome their negative feelings about school. Whether students had been successful or not in their prior academic endeavors, most emphasized the tedium, irrelevance, and general unpleasantness of school. The consensus among the students in the sample was that school is definitely not fun. Accordingly, such students viewed college as necessary to their long-term aspirations but described it as something to be endured only for its long-term (delayed) benefits.

Sam stated his theory of high school as, "The way I see it, they were just giving a reason to keep a bunch of kids off the streets until they're eighteen or whatever." This view of school accounted for the delay between high school graduation and college entrance because, as he put it, "I had a feeling I'd go to college, but I wasn't sure yet, and I was really sick of high school—as I'm sure everyone is."

Such statements about the drudgery of school echo findings from a large-scale study of adolescents conducted in the 1990s.[2] On the whole, the authors report, students "do not appear to find most of their academic classes interesting or enjoyable. Academic classes are positively associated with challenge and importance to future goals, but they do not foster enjoyment, positive affect, or motivation."

Indeed, most students seem resigned to undergoing a dreadful experience in order to earn the desired credential. Serena related the events of the prior fall semester, when she enrolled at another community college in the state. "I wasn't ready for school yet, and my dad pushed me into it, and I went, but . . . I just wasn't ready for it, and I just didn't feel like I wanted to go to school, because I had just gotten out of school and I was just tired of it."

Consequently, Serena registered for several courses but did not attend any classes; nor did she complete any assignments. Her first semester at LSCC, however, the semester of our interview, Serena reported a big change in her attitude toward college. The previous year, she recalled, "I just didn't like going, I would find every and any excuse not to go to school. And now I don't mind going. I don't *like* going to school, but I don't mind." Serena's solution for being "sick of school" was to postpone full participation until she was "ready." Ready meant, for her, "not minding" college.

Eva's dilemma during her final year of high school reflected a similar view of schooling. "Well, I always said that I was going to college, and then my senior year of high school I was like, 'I'm tired of school. I don't have to go anymore—why am I going to go now?'" In the end, her parents' perspective influenced her decision to matriculate at the local two-year college and "start my basics now so I won't be losing time and not want to start school later on." Once Eva recognized that attending college would not become more appealing as time passed, she decided that she might as well start immediately.

In fact, the distinction between getting an education and enjoying it emerged as a basic theme for the vast majority of students. Joy, for example, who regarded comp as a vital course, drew an explicit distinction between learning from the class and enjoying it.

> The class, I would say, is an excellent class. I think it's a necessary class that all students should have as freshmen, because it prepares you for writing papers in all different classes. Because in all different subjects, you're going to eventually have to write a paper, and this is teaching you how to do that.
>
> It is a necessary evil, pretty much, because I don't know anybody who likes this class, but it's necessary if you want to be successful in your other classes with the papers that you have write. So I like the class on a learning standpoint.
>
> On a fun standpoint, I hate it. No.

POTENTIAL PITFALLS

Balancing short-term considerations and long-term goals was further complicated for students by the potential pitfalls of their chosen career paths. Uncertainty about the future changed the calculus; if students could be assured of the long-term benefits of college, perhaps the short-term costs would be easier to bear. Certainly such pivotal decisions as the most efficient route to career success might be less perilous. As Melanie pointed out, "when it comes to your money and your time, your decisions on life have to be almost 100 percent correct."

Joy, a white woman in her first semester of college, offers a clear example of students' efforts to forestall future problems. Joy, who had graduated from high school the previous spring, targeted criminology as her field of study, asserting, "I want to go into the FBI and be a field officer." This was not her first choice of a career, however. Teaching, she explained, had been her original choice.

> I changed my major. . . . And the reason I changed to what I'm going into now is because they don't pay enough and I don't want to be living from paycheck to paycheck.
>
> I think, honestly, after I finish the career that I'm going into, I will ultimately go into teaching afterwards, because I don't think I'd want to fully retire until I actually need to because I'm old. But I think that would be what I do *afterwards,* once I have financial stability.

Especially after seeing her recently divorced mother struggle financially, Joy was trying to outline a practical career path. And though she envisioned teaching as her true vocation, thinking about the realities of maintaining financial stability had altered her educational and occupational plans. Not only had Joy modified her degree objectives, but she had also decided against attending a four-year college for all her baccalaureate coursework. Attending a two-year college, she explained, would enable her to save a lot of money before transferring and earning a baccalaureate from the state university.

Whereas attaining a financially secure future was of utmost importance to students, selecting a satisfying occupation was not something they dismissed. Clay, for example, explicitly asserted that he wanted more than just a good job. In fact, he attributed the purely instrumental perspective to his parents, contrasting it with his own rationale for college. "My parents have influenced me, definitely—but I kind of take that with a grain of salt, because it's almost like their reason for getting an education is so I can get a good job to make money and be happy, when my reason for getting an education is learning to do something that I would like to do, and further myself that way, rather than furthering the way that I present myself, like saying, 'Hey, I have a degree.'"

For Clay, attending college meant more than obtaining the

credential or than being able to say, "Hey, I have a degree." Sarah illustrated a similar attitude when she described her lingering doubts about her chosen career trajectory. She worried that she was preparing for a career that would prove to be unsatisfactory in some crucial yet unanticipated way. Essentially, she did not want to spend precious resources for a commodity that would later prove unnecessary. "My biggest fear is just going to school for four to six years, and then getting my degree, and going out into the field doing that. And then I hate it, and I've wasted six years of doing something. Then I've been going to school for something I don't want to do anymore. So that's my fear."

Sarah's fundamental conception of college highlights its function in occupational certification. At the end of the process, changing her career would presumably invalidate the education that prepared or certified her to do the originally intended job.

Sarah's experience at the community college fostered this narrow view of utility. Upon matriculating at LSCC, students met with an adviser and created a degree plan, as well as a first-semester course schedule based on their choice of major. Students who were undecided about their majors were sent to the career counseling center, where they could explore their interests, connect them to possible careers, and then decide on their LSCC major. Thus, from the moment they entered LSCC, students were encouraged to view their degree plans (and specific course requirements) as directly linked to a particular career path. Furthermore, for students who aimed to obtain specific occupational credentials, from certification in Cisco (computer networking) to early childhood care, it was not clear that the technical knowledge gained in earning the credential would transfer to a different career path. In this context, each decision imposed constraints on future paths. At least, students understood them as constraints, and voiced worry about the long-term implications of various choices.

Whereas students like Joy and Sarah thought carefully about the end result of their career choice, others worried about what might happen along the way. Charmaine, who had decided to earn her associate's degree without accumulating any extra transfer credits, was one such student. She alluded to the possible pitfalls in explaining why she wasn't pursuing her long-term goal as directly as possible. Instead, she had developed an intermediate goal, just in case: "I want to at least get the associate, so if something happens . . . at least I will have the associate's degree. I'll have something."

Talisha, a student in her early twenties, mentioned the family issues and financial exigencies that had determined the path she took to college. Outlining the chronology of events, she noted that her family had moved to the Southwest from New York; then "a whole lot of stuff happened, so school—it kind of got put back, just because the situation was fuzzy." The situation was fuzzy, in part, because Talisha spent some time seeking full-time employment, first as a pharmacy technician in training, then as a nurse's aide. About her future educational and career plans, Talisha told me, "Right now, I'm doing the prereqs for the nursing program. And my long-term goal is kind of, totally off that path. It's actually—I want to go into law. . . . I always wanted to do law, the only thing that changed is the kind of law. . . . for a long time I wanted to do criminal law, then I changed it to business law." The law, however, was a dream that Talisha had postponed because of her family. "I work at Southwest Medical Center as a nurse's aide, so having worked in that field and seeing all that's going on, it would be—I don't want to say it would be easy, but—it would be the more commonsense thing to do, to hurry up and finish and get some type of base work established, and then progress to what I am interested in from there. So I'm going to use nursing as a footstool, so I can have that fallback. I mean, that kind of sucks, but that's the honest truth." Talisha viewed nursing as a "more commonsense thing to do" because it would allow her to establish an employment base that would serve as both a fallback and a "footstool." Nursing, though it might enable Talisha to establish herself in the workforce, did not advance her toward her true vocational goal (the law). Like Joy, who chose criminal justice over teaching, Talisha deferred her dream in order to pursue what she perceived as the financially practical course.

Woven through students' accounts was a common thread: Regardless of how detailed students' plans may have been, the vagaries of fate or luck could divert them from their aims at any point. Both Talisha and Joy suggested that they would someday reach their eventual goals in spite of such detours.

Others, however, suggested that it is unrealistic to expect to control the future. Yolanda spoke of such detours as forks or bumps in the road and equated decision-making opportunities with rolls of the dice.

> Now that I'm in school, I may flunk half of the classes that I'm in this year. I mean, it just may happen that way. I may just pass one out of the four. . . . You win some, you lose some.
>
> In a sense, life is out of your control. You know, you never know what's going to happen. I mean, a sickness in the family can occur. . . . You can't help that. You may miss a class. You may get behind. . . . You have all this other outside stuff. Either you work more hours and pay for your stuff. Or you take these classes and go crazy with credit card debt. And then you get your education and then the money that you spent to get your education—when you find a good-paying job, you lose all your money paying off these people you owe.
>
> So that's what I mean by it's a lose-win situation. You never know what's going to happen. You can be organized all you want to, but . . . there's something that's always going to fall behind.

COST-BENEFIT ASSESSMENTS

All these examples illustrate the strength of students' convictions regarding the importance of college. The impetus to attend college and earn a degree was powerful enough for them to justify applying valuable—and often scarce—resources toward that end. Furthermore, in the face of past detours, delays, or failures and with an awareness of the potential for disruptions in the future, students demonstrated a high regard for efficiency, and they considered strategies to win, while minimizing the consequences of losing.

JENN

Since "about ninth grade," Jenn had had the idea that she would become an elementary school teacher; however, she changed her mind because of the amount of schooling required. Missing the irony, she told me, "I'm not a big school person, and education is what I really want to do, but being in school all day just doesn't really appeal to me. You know, to come and do all that work." Once she enrolled in college, she did some research and found out that she could go into interpretation for the deaf, which would allow her to work in schools but would require one less year of schooling. She found a college in Arkansas with bachelor's degrees in interpretation for the deaf, and switched her "entire major over" at the community college, so that she would be able to transfer. Finally, she got up the nerve to tell "Mama" about her new plan.

What also becomes clear from these accounts of a range of diverse students is that a shared economic framework shaped their assessments of college: it comprised decisions about continuing college, dropping out, changing plans, and approaching specific coursework in individual courses. Ultimately, the costs and potential pitfalls of higher education led students to question whether they were really making the best choices and to express doubt about the net usefulness of college attendance. Most frequently, they couched their concerns in the language of economics—getting the biggest bang for the buck.

Melanie entered college with plans to become a psychologist. Midway through her first semester, she was deeply disappointed by the field of psychology as represented in her introductory courses.

When I first started [at LSCC], and I first started listening to the lectures and everything, it was really boring, and I kind of had a small little crack in my foundation, because I didn't know if I wanted to do psychology anymore, because it was so bland and so boring; it was so [pause] generic. But I guess, as I progress into the field of psychology, there will be branches into different sections, and I will choose my life at that branch.

I am good at psychology and understand the concepts, but I guess I just have to wait until they start narrowing it down, and I start figuring out the part of psychology that I want to go into.

I guess you just have to deal with a lot of b.s., and then get to the good stuff.

Wistfully, she noted, "I just wish I didn't have to go through the college experience, and just get my job—my ideal job—and just skip all this stuff and just get a job and live my life." For Melanie, who viewed college as a requirement for her career aspirations, higher education served simultaneously as the means of achieving her goal and as an obstacle to starting a job and getting on with her life.

MELANIE

Describing herself as "way too analytical" and a "little neurotic," Melanie also explained why the idea of going into psychology had such appeal for her. "I think—okay, this is just my theory—anyone who chooses to go into a field of psychology, or go into psychiatry, they ultimately make that decision because they want to find out who they are, and how they react to the world, and how the world reacts to their actions. People who go into this field are very—are automatically going to think on an upper level. It doesn't mean that they're more intelligent, or that they're geniuses, it's just they tend to think from a different angle than the way society thinks."

In assessing the value of specific courses, "getting [their] money's worth" emerged as students' primary criterion. Accordingly, the issue of financial cost emerged in both real and figurative terms, as part of the pervasive economic metaphor for assessing value. Hugh, for example, sized up his math class by asserting, "Compared to the other courses that I have, in my math course, I'm getting what I'm paying for—getting a whole lot out of it." Similarly, Yolanda discussed the value of her precollege math class by referring to the cost of the textbook. "I've always been weak in math, so it's a struggle for me. But him—as a teacher—if I had to rate him? An excellent job. For the book being $127 for a class I'm not even going to get credit for, it breaks it down and it lets me know what I missed in school." In this math class, noted Yolanda with a mixture of surprise and pride, she was finally beginning to understand math. Thus she considered the high cost of the textbook to have been worth it.[3]

Mariella, who had entered the community college with a "good attitude," as she herself described it, was disappointed by most of her classes. As a result, by the end of her first semester, she was reassessing her educational objectives. "I don't enjoy school. I don't really think it brings anything to me, to be honest. So I kind of—that's why I have this whole negative attitude. To be honest with you, I'm just in school to have some kind of career."

For Mariella, school had never been fun or enjoyable—but simply something to get through. Had there been no expectation on the part of her parents that she attend college and pursue a career, Mariella assured me, she would not have enrolled in any college courses. Mariella wondered aloud whether she might be just as happy working as a 911 dispatcher. She reflected, "And I know fifteen dollars an hour is not a lot. But what is a lot?" Mariella's experience of her first-semester courses at LSCC prompted her to question her original decision to attend college and earn a degree. In light of her comments at the end of that semester, it is not surprising that her commitment to the associate's degree plan had waned, or that she was reconsidering her original goal of becoming a "professional" of some sort.

In retrospect, she concluded that she had wasted money on all but one of her courses that semester. Upon matriculation at LSCC, she had initially selected an associate's degree plan in criminal justice in consultation with an academic adviser. Later, she discovered from her classmates that she could earn a certificate in criminal justice instead of an associate's degree. She would not be required to take core courses such as Comp 1, Introduction to Psychology, or math to earn the certificate. "I would just be taking those classes in that field. . . . so I would have been done in maybe just two semesters. And then I would have had a certificate. I would have been able to go into the field and then come to school and take the stupid [core] classes later. But I wasn't told that, and I had to pay for classes, which—it wasn't a whole lot or anything—I would have just rather paid for a class I wanted to take." For Mariella, earning the certificate rather than the degree offered an appealing means of improving her occupational prospects, particularly because the only course she reported enjoying that semester was also the only one required for the certificate. Although willing to pay money to take the essential classes, she voiced irritation at the wastefulness of paying for courses that she deemed useless and unenjoyable. In other words, although Mariella indicated that the cost of attending college was not a problem for her in the sense of her actually being able to pay the tuition, the financial metaphor offered a powerful means of expressing the value (or lack thereof) of her courses.

Liz was the student who offered the most extreme version of this utilitarian perspective: that college was important primarily as it applied to her occupational and financial future, and that the best college experience was the shortest one. She outlined her plan to complete as much transferable coursework as possible at the community college and then attend a nearby campus of the state's four-year college system. "That way, when I do go to State, it's not that big of a waste of money; I'm just taking classes I need to take. I don't need to waste my money on that. I can come here without—I can get a loan, pay it off, or I could just pay it off straight up instead of paying thousands of dollars to get no education whatsoever." Liz acknowledged the importance of the college credential but did not perceive that the college courses had any relevance to her career interest (radio production). In this regard, attending college was not about her "education." Liz did mention one exception: her class called Mass Communications, during which the instructor demonstrated the uses of various kinds of equipment and students had the majority each class session to engage in "hands-on" work. She predicted (or assumed) that her college experiences (both two-year and four-year) would afford her "no education whatsoever." As she had explained earlier, on-the-job experience is the most important and valuable learning experience in her chosen field. As evidence, she cited conversations she had had with experienced people at her job (at a local radio station), who informed her that a college degree was irrelevant for the actual work involved in radio production. Therefore, Liz viewed a college degree as valuable only in terms of what it could be exchanged for.

> I mean, honestly, I could quit right now, and have a career for the rest of my life. I have so much experience in radio that I wouldn't even need a degree. I've talked to people that I work with that, I mean, I was an RTF [Radio-Television-Film] major at Met U, and I talked to my boss, and he said that's a waste of money. . . . He's like, 'Get a business degree, or something else,' so I'm probably going to do public relations or business or something. But it's all about experience. Like with audio engineering, if you have experience in that, or experience in radio, or sales, that's all it is. That's really all you need. And the degree's just like a backup that usually helps when you're getting a job, because I know various people that have degrees that have absolutely nothing to do with their job.

Liz thus decided to major in business merely to obtain an academic credential; she was convinced she would get "no education" for her career in radio. The underlying problem for her was the limited applicability of a business degree—or any other course of study—to her chosen field. From her point of view it was not worth gaining skills and knowledge not directly applicable to her specific career path, or as she asked, referring to the general education core courses, "What's the point?" She saw no reason to learn "a lot of stuff you don't use."

Perhaps if there *were* an obvious relationship between college courses and her career goals, then paying "thousands of dollars" would be worthwhile, but "why waste your money?" Liz didn't anticipate finding anything intrinsically appealing about her college education: "I figure by the time I've done three years of college already, I'll be ready to get out. Regardless of how hard it is. Just get it over with."

Note that Liz's prior postsecondary experiences complicated her assessment of the value of college attendance. After attending Metropolitan University the previous year, Liz had been placed on academic probation. Rather than continue there, she enrolled in classes at the nearby community college as her "alternative solution." In describing her trajectory to the community college, she said: "I got to the university and I realized that I didn't want to be there, nor was that the place I needed to be. It was too overcrowded. The classes were terrible. None of my teachers spoke English." Liz asserted that she had attended a "shitty high school" and that she was completely unprepared for the work at Met U. More important, she disliked every class. She offered numerous critiques of the professors, the instruction format (the classes held in huge auditoriums), the course content, and even her course schedule.

Liz described her pursuit of efficiency in the most matter-of-fact terms, and she was far from alone in her desire to complete college as quickly as possible. "Getting it over with" was a wish that students expressed in all kinds of contexts: in reference to college attendance, to taking specific courses, and to completing particularly irksome assignments. Students proffered numerous examples of specific courses they were taking or had taken in which the subject matter, the teaching, or the specific assignments were useless.

Throughout these examples, students buttressed their assessments of the value of the education they were receiving in economic terms. Indeed, getting their money's worth emerged as students' primary criterion, part of the pervasive economic metaphor for assessing value. The issue of financial cost loomed large in both real and figurative ways. Students frequently referred to higher education as a potential waste of resources, and they described their efforts not to waste time, the need to save money, and the desire to get the most for their money.

Decisions about when and whether to attend college therefore depended in part on a complicated cost-benefit analysis, in which students weighed the potential long-term economic benefits of the degree against the extent to which they would be "wasting" time and money while earning the degree.

Most telling in this context is the decision that Susan came to in reconsidering her psychology plan. "Well, that's when I decided, 'Do I really want to go to Cal State? Do I really want to go to a four-year college?' I'm kind of sick of this; I'm already over it and it's only been three years. And psychologists: I'd have to go to school for like, endless amounts, and then there's the Ph.D., and there's just too much involved with it." Without the motivation to pursue a degree in psychology, Susan questioned her continued attendance at the community college: "Why do I have to sit around here and learn things that I don't want to learn, or spend my parents' money on things that I'm not going to use?" Describing the community college as "a dead end," she presented her new idea, to enter the Fashion Institute and Design Merchandising (FIDM), "a trade school, where I actually want to be something." Even though FIDM would be "really expensive," she wouldn't have to "just sit at HCC and get no rewards whatsoever." Susan acknowledged that she had had "really good grades" at HCC, but that didn't matter: grades were not the kind of reward she was seeking.

For these students, higher education represented an investment in their future, and they wanted some assurance that their education would pay off—in the literal sense. Short-term choices therefore took on great importance, and decisions students made about matriculation, degree plans, and course taking were guided by their concern over using scarce resources—time and money— in the most efficient and effective way.

Perhaps most important, this perspective shaped their approach to coursework and students' interactions with faculty. In the next chapter I explore how the desire for a "useful" education complicates students' learning opportunities.

CHAPTER 4

"HOW IS THAT HELPING US?"

REBEKAH NATHAN, in her account of the year she spent living like a first-year college student, describes a critical revelation. She explains that as a college professor she had an incomplete understanding of students that often led her to address classroom problems in ways that were bound to fail. Only after her "freshman year" investigating students' behavior and intentions more closely did she finally recognize this truth. "I could see why my former 'solutions' had not changed [students'] behavior. Like many of my teaching and administrative colleagues, I often design solutions to student problems that do not address the actual source of th-e problem. The miscalculations come from faulty assumptions concerning what good students do and how they organize their academic lives."[1] So too have my own studies of college students clarified how professors' best intentions can go awry, and underscored the need to probe beneath the surface of students' performance. The earlier chapters illustrate how students' preconceptions and expectations inevitably complicate the dynamics of teaching and learning in college classrooms. Professors may craft solutions that miss the mark; just as easily, students may not understand the "solution" as it is intended.

Given students' pragmatic approach to education as a means to achieve their career goals and their efforts to avoid wasting time or money, it would be easy to imagine that these students cared about earning the credential but were not much concerned with learning. A superficial look at their approach to coursework suggests that students were attempting to "succeed at school without really learning," as the education historian David Labaree put it.[2] A more thorough examination of students' orientation to college, however, reveals that students sincerely hoped to learn something important and meaningful in college. At the same time, their understanding of important and meaningful information was tightly linked to practical goals, and it reflected rather narrowly defined conceptions of knowledge and learning. More than once I have spoken to students who questioned their professors' typical instructional strategy. They ask, "How is that supposed to help me?" As we have seen, when students determine that their learning goals are not being realized, they tend to rethink their postsecondary plans altogether or to just want to "get it over."

MAKING THE GRADE

Regardless of a student's academic background, career aspirations, or level of interest in the subject matter, the grading procedures in each class exert a huge influence on everyone's approach to the coursework. Typically, students' highest priority is to satisfy the instructor's criteria for passing the course. As Mariella put it, "I have to pass the class, in order to have a good grade point average, in case I do ever want to transfer. Not necessarily a good GPA—but I have to do what [the professor] tells us to do, so I can pass the class, so I can get somewhere."

Even the most self-confident and academically accomplished students mentioned the centrality of grades in the learning process. Luis, a self-described "serious" and highly motivated student, was one of the few who identified himself as both well prepared for college and knowledgeable about it. When Luis explained how his high school experience had prepared him for college, he stated, "I was very prepared, because my junior and senior years I had a lot of AP courses. And so we had college-level work to do, and most of the time my teachers actually acted like college professors. They didn't really care about your grade, they just let you go—and if you failed a test, that's too bad. So I didn't feel like nervous about college. I was actually excited." In framing the relationship between professor and students, Luis contended that professors don't really care about students' grades or whether students fail. From this perspective, the task of objectively evaluating college students' performances both supersedes concern with outcomes and places the full responsibility for passing the course on students. This aspect of the college experience, Luis suggests, is the one that elicits the most anxiety from students. A student named Clay expressed this point more explicitly: "I think some people are intimidated by their professors, because they control their grades. And they don't want to look like a fool, because they don't understand a subject, or maybe they have asked before, they didn't really get an explanation, and they don't want to come back and ask the same question."

Clay, who had initially started college at the state's flagship university, did not consider himself a typical community college student. He thought of himself as savvier, more capable of meeting high academic standards than many of his peers at the community college. This attitude came through when he talked about how much other students fear writing. In speaking about those who feel intimidated, he describes what he sees as typical community college students but does not include himself in that category.

The grading system for each course directs students to focus their attention on the material they deem essential to completing graded assignments. Passing each course, and remaining a college student, are dependent on the student's understanding what the instructor plans to assess and the exact assessment procedures. In every classroom, this need leads to demands for nitty-gritty logistical and procedural details about the course assess-ments.[3] When students do not believe that they have enough information about the grading criteria or about the instructor's guidelines for a particular assignment, I have seen them ask—and ask and ask—what often appear to be petty questions about minutiae. The sociologist Howard Becker has called this ap-proach "making the grade."[4]

Indeed, students at every level of education are faced with grading systems that reward a grade-focused approach to their courses: figuring out what each instructor expects when it comes to graded performance, and how to meet the expectations most efficiently. Howard Becker and his coauthors have termed this the GPA perspective. They contend that it derives from students' acceptance of the rules handed down to them by administrators and faculty. "The student emphasis on grades arises, then, in re-sponse to an academic environment that also emphasizes grades. In a relationship of subjection in which the higher echelon dic-tates what will be institutionalized as valuable, making and en-forcing rules to implement that choice, members of the lower echelon must, if they are to act effectively and remain members of the organization, accept that judgment and shape their own actions accordingly."[5]

Thus, the strategies that students adopt to make the grade, such as allocating most of their effort to graded assignments, seeking information about the grading criteria, and trying to ne-gotiate over instructors' grading decisions, are common re-sponses to a fundamental condition of schooling.

Becker, Geer, and Hughes first explored this perspective in great detail in their study of medical school students at the Uni-versity of Kansas. Throughout the study, they document how the assessment system at the medical school penalized students who targeted their study efforts at the information they thought would be most relevant to their future practice as doctors. Stu-dents needed to study selectively, because the volume of material to learn was entirely unmanageable. Hence, selecting the correct material to study was vital to academic success. But in the end the students who earned the best grades employed a different criterion for directing their study efforts—they relied on the instructor to define what would be tested. In that context, the success of medical students was predicated on their determining the instructor's expectations for each graded assignment.[6]

The bottom line for students everywhere is to save time and find the "clearest and most authoritative source of knowledge," even though it means losing patience with information that is "not both easily grasped and concrete."[7] Students therefore depend on instructors to explain which information will count in graded assessments and to clearly delineate the grading criteria for those assessments.

Ultimately, students' primary objective in each course—to do what the instructor tells them to do in order to get the grade—shapes their conceptions of useful knowledge and the best strategies for gaining that knowledge. The course material that students across different colleges deemed significant tended to take the form of factual, testable knowledge—the kind of knowledge that Colleen referred to as "informative information." Speaking of the assistance she had received at the writing lab, she described the two most helpful tutors by saying, "They're fresh, they have lots of ideas, they have informative information for you." Colleen's phrasing reflected a view shared by her peers: some course material is not informative, some course material is informative, and students must identify and learn the informative kind.

Students' desire to absorb the "informative information" in an efficient manner led to several common critiques of instruction. Some criticisms focused on the volume of information provided in class. These resulted from two kinds of experiences: feeling bombarded with details without knowing how to distinguish the essential facts (what would be tested), or perceiving the instruction as failing to provide enough factual information. In either case, the underlying assumption of students' critiques was that instruction should be both efficient and "informative." James's take on bad instruction, for instance, centered on his instructor's inefficiency in presenting relevant information. "My psychology teacher, sometimes he gives an example of what we are saying with his own experience of what happened outside, so he uses outside information to address the question you have . . . ; so sometimes, what he says doesn't matter to what we are saying in class. And sometimes he repeats something over and over, so I'm like, 'Okay, we had that before, so you don't have to repeat it again.'"

For James, useful knowledge comprised the facts that would appear on the test. From this perspective, inefficient and useless instruction included anything additional, whether that information went beyond the essential facts, represented "outside," experiential knowledge, or simply appeared to James to exist beyond the scope of the textbook. To judge from his own account, James seems to have successfully distinguished which information really "mattered" for the course, and as a result he was easily passing it. He therefore viewed certain instructional strategies—explaining concepts through real-life examples or highlighting critical information through repetition—as both unnecessary and inefficient.

Other students who were enrolled in psychology courses but not getting the grades they wanted reported being utterly confused by "outside information." Unlike James, these students were not successfully identifying what would be tested, or how it would be tested. Mariella, for example, interpreted much of the activity during class sessions as the sharing of opinions and personal stories.

> The professor just kind of gives us objectives and she doesn't really discuss the book. I'm not asking for her to do that. But at least talk about something that the class has to do.

Then on tests, she tests us about stuff that's in the book, but then she comes up with her own stuff. For example, she gives an example of a person, and asks, 'Would a behavioral psychologist treat this?' So she kind of comes out with brand-new things. And a lot of people are lost in that class, too.

It goes back to how they give their own opinions, or they teach us what they think is right. . . . and it's not really a class. Do you know what I mean? I came in here thinking I was going to learn something.

The only classes I feel that I learned something is in math and in criminal justice. Because, for example, my criminal justice teacher, he just kind of gives us notes up there and that's our test. Right. And then I understand it.

Mariella's perspective on textbooks was more flexible than other students' ("I'm not asking her to [discuss the book]"). Nevertheless, she articulated the widespread notion that the important course material is information that it is factual and concrete. She cited two courses, math and criminal justice, in which the tested information consisted largely of rules and other concrete data that can be memorized. Moreover, clear instruction was given in the criminal justice course, where the instructor wrote notes on the board, then tested the students on that information. This instructional approach is good, according to Mariella: as she explained, "Then I understand it." In her psychology class, however, Mariella's instructor solicited discussion of personal stories and opinions—none of which constituted important knowledge in Mariella's eyes. Moreover, she thought, the instructor constructed confusing tests, in asking for responses that went far beyond the concrete facts. By offering a profile of an individual and asking students, "Would a behavioral psychologist treat this person?" the instructor was asking students to apply their knowledge of psychology, but Mariella viewed this kind of question as requiring "brand-new" information.

Mariella appreciated her math course and her criminal justice course because she viewed the information as objectively true, applicable to other classes in the same field, and transferable to practical situations. For her, the rules of algebra and the law functioned as unchanging facts, as opposed to the professor's "opinion" (as she saw the material presented in psychology or English). Ultimately, for Mariella and her peers, the most valuable material she could learn consisted of the facts: those recorded in textbooks, in PowerPoint presentations, or on the blackboard. Because these facts, they assumed, would be assessed on tests, students understood the primary goal of most classes as transcribing those facts for later memorization.

Ryan's description of his government course offers another typical example of this perspective. He identified it as his favorite course and added, "I don't know about enjoying it, but it's— he's a good teacher." When pressed to explain the good aspects of the government instructor's approach, Ryan said, "His lectures correlate a lot with the test, which is kind of rare in some of these classes. He just teaches the material good. I mean, he's organized. He has his notes on PowerPoint, and you can go on his website and print them out before class, and those are the notes that he goes over in class, so you can just follow along with him. You're kind of preexposed to them, so it's a lot easier. [The notes] usually have everything that you need on them, but . . . if it's not on there, you just write it in." In Ryan's mind, the three features of good instruction were clear and organized presentation of information, distribution of PowerPoint handouts matching the lecture slides, and the straightforward assessments by the instructor of students' knowledge ("His lectures correlate a lot with the test"). Although Ryan couldn't say that he actually enjoyed the class, he viewed the course as one that provided the necessary facts in an efficient (organized) manner.

JENN

Throughout the semester that I sat in on Jenn's English class, I observed the classroom activities from my usual seat at the back of the classroom. From the first week of class, Jenn sat in the seat at the end of the second row, against the wall. At the desk immediately in front of her sat Matt, and every class session I observed Matt and Jenn engage in whispered conversations, on what seemed like an ongoing basis. Throughout the semester, I wondered about them. Had they struck up a friendship based on being in the same class together? Were they conferring about course-related matters, or were they just shooting the breeze? Either way, were they paying attention to the class?

I had my chance to find out near the end of the semester, when I interviewed Jenn. I asked her what she and her friend Matt talked about in class. Jenn's answer was a total surprise. Matt was far from being a friend; he always initiated the conversation, and she didn't want to talk to him at all. "He likes to talk. He's like, 'I'll sit there and talk to you.'" She didn't really even respond to Matt, she asserted, he just kept talking to her. And it continued, she told me, because she just "didn't have it in" her to tell him to stop talking to her. With this explanation, Jenn was transformed immediately from a student bold enough to whisper through an entire class session into an entirely different person: an intensely shy woman, too timid to ask her classmate to stop bothering her, in part because "he likes to talk."

From my interview with Jenn, I learned that she was far from disengaged from her English course. English was her favorite class that semester, and since she didn't really respond to Matt's whispered comments, she didn't think he distracted her attention from learning how to write. Indeed, she was supremely pleased with how much she had learned, noting, "That's probably the only English class I've ever enjoyed in my whole entire life, and I've learned a hell of a lot more than I have in my whole years of school. . . . Oh yeah, I definitely learned how to do a lot of things I didn't know how to do before."

"GETTING IT OVER"

All students wanted to make the grade efficiently. The grade each student aimed for, however, varied from course to course, depending on the subject matter, the value the student placed on the objectives of the course, and its relevance to the student's career goals. In the end, if a student concluded that the coursework offered no "useful" knowledge, then "getting it over with"—doing only the minimal work required for a passing grade—proved paramount. In other words, students all hoped to "get the grade"; the decision to exert minimal effort meant doing only enough work to "*just* get the grade."

Students usually began new courses with some sense of the potential for learning. When students viewed an area of study as pertinent to their chosen occupation, their initial approach to the coursework was hopeful: they were hopeful of learning important and usable information. The desire to learn something relevant may exist at the heart of any students' efforts: "Why do we have to learn this?" might be one of the most familiar questions middle school and high school teachers hear.

At times, however, students are certain that particular courses will offer them nothing of use. In such instances, students adopt the "get it over" strategy from the outset of the course. This is often the case, certainly, for students pursuing specialized technical fields, such as computer networking or engineering, who enroll in general education courses. Indeed, some students have a pretty narrow interpretation of "useful." Liz, for example, the student who aspired to a career in radio production (and was working part-time at a local radio station), insisted that her math and English courses were a complete waste of time. She already knew enough math to get along in life—she could balance her checkbook without difficulty—and she certainly had no plans to write essays as part of her career. The only course she described as worthwhile was Mass Communications, which she viewed as immediately practical. As for the other courses, however, her attitude, as we saw in Chapter 3, was, "What's the point? There's a lot of stuff you don't use, so what's the point of learning it?"

Ryan's description of the college's general education requirements (the basic classes) reflected the same definition of worthwhile subject matter. "I think right now, everybody—like, during their freshman, sophomore year of college—they take a bunch of basic classes, and so there's a bunch of those that you're not really interested in. And then, once you get later on, like maybe junior or senior year, you get more specific classes to your major, and then you enjoy those more."

In composition courses, which were structured around the premise that the revision process would improve students' writing skills, the "get it over" strategy seriously undermined that learning opportunity. For instance, Linda's approach to revising her essays consisted of carefully making every change that her teacher recommended, completing each assignment as quickly as possible, and eventually passing the course with a C. When Linda admitted in her interview that she tried to incorporate changes into her papers even when she didn't understand them, I asked whether she ever asked her teacher to explain those comments. "I never [pause] no" was Linda's answer. "I just correct them and I just get it over and get it accepted—'Accept my paper and let's go,'—that's it. That's the class. I don't care, as long as I pass it." After all, she added, "I don't plan to be an English major."

Kevin adopted a slightly different strategy in composition. Instead of making every change suggested by his instructor, Kevin operated by asking himself, "What is the *least* amount of change I need to make to get the revised paper accepted?" For instance, on Kevin's first draft of his research paper, his instructor had recommended a series of revisions, including rewriting the introduction, tightening up the thesis statement, removing some irrelevant quotes, eliminating a section with irrelevant citations, and adding topic sentences to each paragraph. Kevin expressed dismay at the feedback, asserting that he did not want to do very much work on the revision. He resisted the idea of eliminating sections, for example, because he feared that his paper would no longer meet the minimum word requirement. Even the idea of moving sentences around struck him as being too much effort, and he reiterated several times, "I just want to get it accepted."

Not every student shared this narrow perspective on the value of English composition. Eliana believed that what she learned in composition could enhance her writing and thinking skills both in and out of school. In addition, she spoke of her engagement with the ideas she encountered in composition class, and how much she appreciated the opportunity to examine issues as matters for debate. There were other students like Eliana, but they were a minority. In general, the vast majority of college students I encountered expressed the "get it over" attitude toward at least one of their courses. The attitude manifests itself in minimal effort, disengagement, and, most likely, minimal learning.

The most unfortunate aspect of this widespread approach is that so many students adopted it after enrolling in particular courses; many of the students who spoke of frustration or disenchantment with their coursework indicated that they had made the decision to work merely for a passing grade only after the course failed to meet their expectations.

Students' initial orientations—and their judgments about whether particular courses would offer something worth learning—were subject to change over the span of each semester. In instances when a student entered a course with a pessimistic attitude about its value, a positive experience could change his mind. Sam was one such student—in his case, he experienced a marked turnaround in his view of college altogether. "Now that I've come here, I've changed my opinion, because I see that they actually teach things in college, whereas they really didn't in high school." During high school Sam felt he was "being pressured to go to a place that is just basically there to waste your time." In contrast, he was not "being pressured to go" to college, and it was turning out to be "a place where you're going to learn something." As he put it, "Not having to go, but then going and seeing that there's education there—it's like an extra thing, . . . it's like two plusses."

Unfortunately, the reverse was far more typical: students entered particular courses with hopeful attitudes—eager, or at least interested in learning something of use during the semester. I found myself surprised at the extent of disappointment that students expressed, and the frequency with which students moved from initial optimism to disillusionment. Ryan, for instance, commented on his psychology teacher, whose lectures contained material that seemed to conflict with information he had learned the preceding year in his AP psychology class. When I asked Ryan whether he had ever asked his instructor about the discrepancies, he replied, "I've thought about saying something that would kind of disprove him, but I just keep quiet, do the work and—yeah, just get the grade."

In the end, some students who worked to get college over with had relinquished any hope of learning. As Paul put it, "I'm not learning anything about history. I just go to class, and I sit there, and I do the assignments. I study when you've got to study for the exam, and that's it." But this was not necessarily true of everyone. Sebastian reflected, "I'm not taking it all in—I know that. . . . I'm just doing the homework to get a grade, it seems like, and I'm getting my grade back. . . . But I guess I'll learn some of that stuff later on."

SEBASTIAN

Sebastian viewed his English courses as eminently useful. This may have been, in part, because they were required, and Sebastian needed to pass them before he would be allowed to take certain college-level courses. For Sebastian, the desire to learn was directly related to being "motivated." He characterized himself as "pretty motivated," though he noted that his level of commitment during high school had been very low. "Because I got this lack of motivation in me. It's getting better. It was really bad in high school; I wouldn't care about anything. . . . Like, I never really read a book before. In high school, I just read the Cliff Notes, or whatever; I never read the books. And when I did, they were so boring."

Sebastian felt engaged by and interested in his current courses, in contrast to his high school experience. In addition, he described both his English classes as requiring commitment if students were to do well. For him, that meant reading the books in his basic reading skills course, keeping up with the homework in his writing skills course, and in general, wanting more than to *just* get a grade. In the case of his writing course, he would recommend the course and the professor to those who shared his commitment: "I'd recommend Mr. Burke to someone else; I'd recommend him to someone who's motivated about school, and they wanted to learn—then I'd say, 'Take this guy, because he can help you out.' Someone who just wanted a grade, wanted to get by: I wouldn't take that class at all." In his own case, Sebastian had stuck with the course because he didn't want just to "get by."

On the surface, the two most common approaches, getting the grade and getting it over (or "*just* getting the grade") seem to illustrate a disheartening pattern of student disengagement and lack of interest in real learning. Indeed, they could easily be attributed to students' lack of motivation and jaded response to schooling or interpreted as the inevitable consequence of grading systems that provide incentives for students to expend as little thought and energy as possible in fulfilling the requirements.[8]

Yet in fact these approaches emerged from students' best and most sincere efforts to learn something in college. Although students approached courses with the single-minded goal of getting an acceptable grade, they didn't necessarily view efforts to "make the grade" as distinct from learning the subject matter. On the contrary, students exhibited idealism about the connection between learning and earning grades. At times, students seemed to depend on the grading system to promote learning. Felicia, for example, spoke disparagingly of the pass-fail writing assignments in her composition course. She criticized the incentive structure of pass-fail grading.[9] "I don't like it because you write the essay, but if you do better than C [pass], you still just get the pass. . . . It doesn't really make you think, 'I've got to try my best.' Like, on most essays you try your best, write the best you can, but this one, it's like you can try your best, but you're only going to get a pass." Instead of encouraging students to meet minimum standards, Felicia argued, tests and essays should challenge students to learn at a higher level.

In fact, as Becker, Geer, and Hughes have contended, working to "get the grade" offers the most efficient strategy for studying. Because the grading system indicates what the instructor thinks is the most important material to learn, detailed instructions about each assignment (and the grading criteria) help students distinguish between essential and secondary material and eliminate the guesswork about how to study. Furthermore, attending to activities and assignments that do not "count" in the final grade may very well be a waste of time. With no certain reward, students may wonder, why risk it?

Talisha experienced her history class as a waste. Reporting the disappointment she felt with the learning afforded by the class, she explained, "It's so annoying. I found out like two, three weeks ago—no, I found out like a month ago—that his lecture didn't count, and I kept coming in hopes that something would be revealed to me, some spit of knowledge would be imparted into my soul. But every time he opens the book, give me about thirty minutes, then I'm asleep without fail, because I'm just bored. I'm already tired."

Talisha's efforts to go above and beyond what was required were not rewarded with enhanced learning or greater knowledge. Her perception served to reaffirm for her the widely held notion that learning results primarily from energy expended on graded assignments and activities.

In light of students' fears (see Chapter 2) and their desire to succeed in school and "get somewhere" in life (Chapter 3), students are pressured to figure out exactly what they need to do to pass each graded assignment. For students who go into college without much notion of the standards and expectations for college-level work, receiving specific guidelines for each assignment becomes even more critical. This need is heightened when students perceive each professor as promoting different standards. Mariella identified the problem when she described professors as all having different teaching styles—each one seemingly teaching what he or she "thinks is right." Mariella appeared especially concerned because of past experiences in school: teachers didn't really teach anything ("except for elementary, because teachers really teach you there"). From her perspective, she had "been cheated from education" in her previous encounters with school.

In the case of composition, she explained how "different styles" might cause problems.

> What is really right for a good paper? Everybody has their standards. So if Mr. Dobbs is teaching me, and he thinks this is a good paper, then what if I do what he told me to do, and I take it to another professor and maybe that's not his standards? And if my teacher says, 'Well, it's not a good paper,' what am I supposed to do?
>
> So what is right? So that's very vague; there's no curriculum—I mean, is that what all the teachers think is a good paper? Or is that just his opinion? Do you know?

If Mariella does not gain absolute, concrete knowledge from her coursework, then what has she learned, and how will she succeed in the next class?

Her complaint is directly related to the typical undergraduate student's experience, which Gerald Graff describes as being tossed around in a disconnected, incoherent curriculum. For many students, he contends,

> the curriculum represents not a coherent intellectual world with conventions and practices anyone can internalize and apply to the specific challenges of each discipline, but an endless series of instructors' preferences that you psych out, if you can, and then conform to, virtually starting over from scratch in each new course. Some instructors want you to recall and give back information without interpretation or judgment, whereas others want you to express your own

ideas. Some instructors think there are clear-cut answers to questions, whereas others (often in the same discipline) think there are no right answers and that those who think so are naïve or authoritarian.[10]

Consequently, the most effective strategy for "psyching out" an instructor's preferences is to ask questions about how grades will be assigned and to focus on the graded assignments.

Students' dismissive attitudes toward particular activities arise from their certainty that the activities will not help them with the graded assignments. But it is not necessarily just about the grade. Sarah's complaint centered on one of her classmates in composition, who consistently extended the time spent discussing the assigned readings. "And I understand she wants to sit there, but don't waste my time for forty-five minutes, talking about the same story that we were talking about the moment we walked in the door. I want to learn something. I don't care about the story that we read yesterday. I want to learn something today. So that just irritated me." Sarah's criticism suggests that time spent on activities not tied to graded work is wasted, because it detracts from learning.

Underlying the frustration Sarah expressed was her assumption that learning does not result from engaging in discussion with her peers or listening to such discussion. Sarah conceded that her classmate had the right to talk about the readings—but only for a limited amount of time. In part, this view reflects Sarah's conception of learning as something that happens when the instructor presents the course material. With respect to what counts as useful information, Sarah's complaint highlights a view that every other student also expressed: Course content that appears in the form of instructors' opinions, fellow students' input, or other unverifiable statements is not particularly "informative."

In sum, disengagement on the part of students resulted less

from their not wanting to learn anything than from their convictions about what activities might enable learning. In Mariella's case, she very much wanted to learn how to write a good paper, and she thought that she would do so in composition. Once she determined that she wasn't really learning anything, however, she adopted the "get it over" attitude. "I'm not very concerned, since—this class doesn't make me very happy. So I kind of just go through it, and I don't take a lot of time—my time—for this class. I just write what he told me to write, just to get over it."

By the end of the semester, she had decided, "As long as I pass the class, I don't care. [pause] I shouldn't be having that attitude, but . . ." Mariella attributed what she termed her bad attitude to her frustration with the content and instruction for the composition course. "I care [about doing better than just passing], but I get frustrated to a point that I just don't care anymore."

MELANIE

Even though she wasn't necessarily "the best" student in high school, Melanie enjoyed taking "upper-level" classes, including an Advanced Placement English class during her senior year. She noted, "I just really enjoyed that class so much, because when you're in high-level classes, it's a very relaxed atmosphere, because the teacher already knows that in order to be here, you have to be studious, you have to have determination, and work hard and things like that. And so a lot of the times we would just have discussions on the books that we read over the night, or we would take quizzes and things like that, but I really, really love that kind of upper-level kind of atmosphere." By contrast, though, she explained that she did not apply the same level of determination to all her courses or assignments. When she regarded assignments as stupid or a waste of her time, she didn't bother to try hard. In the case of writing assignments, for example, "I find that if I really believe in something, if I love it enough, then I can write pretty extraordinary, for me, within my confines. But if it's something stupid,

like 'What did you do over the summer?' I kind of give it a half-ass effort. I mean, that's just the way I am."

The most significant aspect of students' disappointment was
not simply the failure to see the relevance of courses—but the
way students conceived of knowledge or meaningful information. From the perspective of college faculty members, some of
these students appear to be entirely clueless. A highly regarded
English professor at a California community college put it most
bluntly: "Of course you get a group of kids who have no conception of what college is all about."

The frequent incidents of student frustration and disillusionment indicate students' desire to learn. Students' understanding
of what is worth learning—as well as how one goes about learning—is the source of much of the difficulty. These conceptions of
college are often incompatible with faculty members' expectations of college students.

What is most problematic about this mismatch of expectations is that students are not generally equipped with the "skills"
or knowledge to determine what their professors expect or how
to meet the expectations. Many community college students
have immense difficulty figuring out how to learn effectively in
specific situations or why they are having trouble with a subject.

Yolanda offers an instructive example. In explaining her criticism of her history professor, who required students to purchase
an expensive text, Yolanda's key complaint hinged on the lack of
assigned readings from the text: "But he doesn't use the book.
And I expressed that to the counselors, and they're like, 'Well,
you know, he should. And maybe next time, keep the book and
see if another teacher is going to use the book, and call the
teacher before you sign up for the class.' That's not my job. My
job is to take the class. His job is to teach. And if he suggests a
book, he needs to let me know before if he's not going to use it."

Yolanda did not conceptualize teaching and learning as an integrated process or as an ongoing interaction between professor and students. Instead, her remarks presupposed a clear separation between professor and students. From her perspective, once the professor has fulfilled his responsibility of explaining and informing, the responsibility moves to the students.

The distinction between the responsibilities of the teacher and the responsibilities of the students also emerged in Mara's interview comments. Trying to explain the source of her difficulty in a prior history class, Mara mused, "Yeah, I don't know. It wasn't like, 'This isn't in the book.' It wasn't like, 'We didn't talk about this in class.' And it wasn't like his lectures weren't really informative. And I really enjoyed his class. I wasn't very good at taking his tests, which is the grade, unfortunately."

In her efforts to determine why the course was difficult for her, Mara ran through a standard list of student grievances, dismissing each possibility in turn. This list revealed her premises about what constitutes bad (and in turn, good) instruction. In other words, the instructor was good, in the sense that (a) his lectures were "really informative," and (b) he didn't introduce questions on the test that were unrelated to the textbook or the lectures. Despite these positive pedagogical features, Mara did not do well in the course, and in the end, she chalked it up to her difficulty with taking the tests. And yet she was unable to explain how or why she had trouble with them. The reasons for her failure remained a mystery, and a better understanding of how to take the tests (and by implication, how to learn) remained beyond her grasp. Mara may have felt responsible for something she did not know how to achieve, but her conception of learning—as something that she alone must accomplish—decreased the likelihood that she would seek the necessary assistance from her instructors.

I do not want to suggest that students share no responsibility for their learning. The way that students like Mara and Yolanda understood the division of responsibility between instructor and student, however, focused their attention on what to learn but not how to learn it. Even more important, their ideas about what to learn were not necessarily congruent with their instructors' assumptions. The following exchange I had with Mariella reinforces this point:

> *Mariella:* Mr. Dobbs does put stuff on the board, and I appreciate that. That's like my enlightenment, when I see that stuff on the board and I write everything down.
>
> *Becky:* Okay. So what would the comp class be like if you were going to learn something from it?
>
> *Mariella:* Well, just maybe like actually have him going on the board and teaching us sometime, not just . . . Like, for example, I don't agree with him the way he gives us out random essays that he finds and other stuff. . . . I would just rather him show us: if it's a Comp 1 class, he's supposed to teach us how to write a good essay.

In contrast to Mariella, I did not view the handouts as "random essays." Rather, the essays provided models of different rhetorical strategies and allowed Mr. Dobbs to illustrate his discussion with specific examples. In addition, some of his selections presented arguments about the value of writing and the power of words. Analyzing the arguments offered students the opportunity to discuss aspects of "argument literacy," as Gerald Graff describes it, while examining a diverse range of opinions on why and how academic literacy affects individuals' lives. In fact, by deconstructing models of good writing, examining the building blocks, and discussing strategies for constructing and combining those building blocks, Mr. Dobbs made a consistent effort to "show" students how to write a good essay. This is not the way Mariella understood the activity, however.

Mariella had hoped to learn something useful from composition—that she was not doing so led her to question the value of the class, as well as the value of earning an associate's degree. By the end of the semester, she complained that she had been advised poorly; she was enrolled in courses that she did not want to take; and a certificate would be a better goal than a degree.

At times, the understanding students have of meaningful, relevant knowledge and how to acquire it leads them to approach course curricula in ways that conflict with instructors' objectives. In some instances—perhaps many—preconceptions lead students to understand the course content and objectives very differently than their professors anticipate. Even when students try to determine instructors' criteria for graded assignments, students' own assumptions about information and relevant knowledge shape the way they interpret (and misinterpret) professors' intentions. The end result is that students' approaches to their coursework frequently differ from what faculty members expect or hope for in class.

In an effective learning environment, part of the instructor's responsibility involves understanding how students perceive the curriculum and the learning objectives and, when necessary, helping students revise their perceptions in a way that supports the instructor's vision of learning. Only then can a teacher close the enormous gap between her expectations and the students' approach to their coursework.

PART 2

CLASSROOM DYNAMICS

THE FUNDAMENTAL MODEL for college teaching can be traced to the end of the nineteenth century, when the American university system as we now know it developed. Professors took on a central institutional role. Instrumental in the discovery of scientific truth—in effect the production of research-based expertise—they were responsible for determining what specialized knowledge was required for practice in the emerging professions. Thus, university faculty members' authority within the college classroom was founded on the knowledge derived from research. As a consequence, their function in the undergraduate college classroom was to transmit that knowledge; professing consisted of organizing and disseminating scientific truths in such a way that students could comprehend them and commit them to memory. The researcher's claim to specialized, expert, and abstruse knowledge distinguished the professor's practice from elementary and secondary school teaching, which had undergone its own redefinition as women's work: feminine, less intellectual, and requiring male supervision.[1]

Professing implied an obligation to scientific truth and to the values of the research process (objective inquiry into the subject matter). Teaching, by contrast, was something akin to child rearing—it entailed an obligation to socialize and civilize children.

The legacy of this construction of teaching along gender lines is reflected in the "semiprofessional" status of teaching below the postsecondary level, as well as in the tendency to underestimate the expertise involved in learning how to teach. The corresponding conception of college instruction—with the attendant assumptions about the role of a professor explaining a specialized field of inquiry, and the responsibility of the student to master the knowledge—has proven highly resistant to change in the field of higher education.

The strength of this model of teaching may be greatest with regard to students' expectations of what will happen in college classes. Earlier chapters have given some indication of what students expect of college professors, such as the presentation of "informative," essential facts and clear explanation of the textbook. In my classroom observations, students seemed wholly comfortable as passive recipients of professors' expert knowledge, in the tradition that the Brazilian educator Paulo Freire labeled a banking approach to education.

This orientation toward teaching and learning generates several kinds of problems for students and, in turn, for professors, as certainly proved true of students in the writing classrooms I observed. In fact, English classrooms may be the site that best illuminates the pedagogical disconnects, because so often the goal is for students to take on authority—at least as the authors of their own writing. In the courses I observed, a sizable number of students complained that they were not being taught how to write. Colleen shed some light on this viewpoint when she told me about her original expectations for the course. "I thought that the professor would tell us how to write papers this semester; then, next semester, in Comp 1B, we would start writing papers."

Not surprisingly, then, one major pedagogical problem arises in classrooms where professors' teaching strategies conflict with the professorial model. This is the issue taken up in Chapter 5, which highlights the negative consequences of this conflict as it played out in two different classrooms. A second major problem emerges from students' own preexisting fears of failing in college, and the tendency of the traditional professorial role to exacerbate avoidance as a student strategy. Chapter 6 highlights the success several professors had in negotiating that tension.

A word about these two chapters: neither one provides an exhaustive account of what happened during the course of the semester inside classrooms. Chapters 5 and 6 do, however, offer a snapshot of several different dimensions of classroom practice and the ways in which students' goals and expectations shape the dynamics of teaching and learning.

CHAPTER 5

COLLEGE TEACHING

As students drifted into the classroom and claimed seats in the rows of desks, several strands of conversation floated in my direction. Allison, seated in a first-row chair, commented favorably on Kelly's jacket ("awesome coat") as Kelly marched into the room. Suzanne had stretched forward across her desk and was whispering her evening plans to Joy, who was seated immediately in front of her. Miguel, Sandra, and Holly quietly watched the scene from seats on the perimeter.

In the few minutes before Lori Brown, the professor, arrived, Kelly introduced a comment about the previous class session, asking with undisguised sarcasm, "Are we all ready for roundtable? Honestly, I feel like I'm back in high school—this is so stupid." Kelly followed up her critique of the roundtable activity by announcing, "I don't feel like she is really teaching us anything."

—Excerpt from field notes, Tuesday, September 10, 2002

AS I WAITED for the fourth session of Professor Lori Brown's composition class to begin, I witnessed the preceding exchange with astonishment. The week before, I had observed Lori deftly facilitate several activities, including an animated and thoughtful group discussion. That she was "teaching" had seemed self-evident to me at the time. After completing the "getting acquainted" exercise begun during session two, Lori directed everyone to move the desks out of the rows into a large circle. Dubbing this form the roundtable, she explained the purpose and guidelines for discussion of the reading assignment, Maya Angelou's "Graduation." For the remainder of the class session, she solicited students' comments on the essay, by employing a set of questions that she promised would build toward a critical analysis of the text. She gently encouraged students to share their thoughts about the assigned reading, after reiterating her expectation that students arrive prepared to participate in class. She asked students to support their assertions with references from the text, and she modeled the practice herself. I was impressed: by the strategies she employed to foster a collaborative environment, by the way she guided students through possible analyses of the text, and by the ease with which she balanced her pedagogical goals.

And yet what I had viewed as skillful pedagogical practice Kelly dismissed with condescension. The connection Kelly drew in her remark between the roundtable format and high school was unmistakably derogatory: for her, highly participatory discussion might be appropriate for high school, but not for college. Kelly assumed that the forms and content of college instruction ought to be clearly distinguished from those used in high school. Her remark "Honestly, I did this in high school" reflected an objection to the focus on students' responses to the assigned reading—as well as to the roundtable pedagogical structure. Ultimately, Kelly's perception that Lori was not "teaching anything" was a function of Lori's pedagogical choice not to present a lecture. Kelly interpreted the absence of a *lecture* as the absence of *instruction*.

Kelly's complaint about the course opened the way for other students to voice criticism until Lori Brown arrived in class. From questions about the "contradictory" directions for the first essay ("I mean, is it three hundred words or five hundred words?") to confusion over submitting revised drafts ("Yeah, I don't really know what's going on with all these drafts and due dates and everything"), this conversation before class revealed a consistent perception that Lori was not providing students with enough information. For these students, Lori was not fulfilling her instructional responsibilities.

This vignette offers a passing glimpse into the conflict that persisted in Lori's class throughout the semester. Fundamentally, the conflict was grounded in opposing conceptions of knowledge and learning, which reflected a tension that exists throughout higher education. Indeed, such comments echo the views expressed by students across a range of postsecondary settings. Consequently, although the extent and intensity of the challenges that arose in Lori's classroom were unusual, they illustrate a problem familiar in teaching practice.

This chapter explores the collisions between students' and instructors' conceptions of teaching that surfaced in two different composition classrooms at a large urban college in the Southwest. During the fall 2002 semester, two instructors, Lori and Beth, taught Comp 1A courses that students perceived as posing explicit challenges to the legitimate (traditional) model of postsecondary instruction.[1] Students' firmly held expectations undermined the instructors' efforts to achieve their pedagogical goals. Ultimately, students' pedagogical conceptions led to overt resistance and prevented them from benefiting from alternate instructional approaches, which they perceived variously as irrelevant "b.s.," a waste of time, or simply a lack of instruction. Similar conceptions have guided students' participation in other classrooms I have observed, but the extent to which, and frequency with which, Lori and Beth flouted the established paradigm for college instruction led to unusually strong resistance from their students. These two cases thus starkly spotlight a phenomenon that is pervasive in college classrooms.

CONCEPTIONS OF TEACHING

Efforts to characterize different orientations toward teaching and learning have resulted in categorizations similar to Paul

Ramsden's three levels of practice. Ramsden's first category, "teaching as telling," characterizes the well-established model of postsecondary instruction and is most commonly associated with the lecture format.[2] The specific instructional format, however, is less noteworthy than the underlying pedagogical goals. In the case of the professorial paradigm, the goal is to clearly transmit knowledge to students. Accordingly, instructors can "profess" in group discussions as well as through lectures. Julie, a faculty colleague of Beth and Lori, frequently facilitated discussions of the assigned readings, for example, during which she solicited students' comments. Sometimes she encouraged everyone to contribute opinions. At other times, Julie limited students' input so that she could explain the material to the students. Indeed, on the first day of class, she noted that when the term "discuss" appeared on the syllabus, it meant that she would "be at the board and tell you exactly what you need to know."

In the second category, which Ramsden terms "teaching as organising," the focus is on experiential learning. In this way of teaching, a teacher may rely on transmitting information, but "telling" plays a subordinate role to supplying hands-on activities in which students participate. The teaching orientation presented in Ramsden's third category (making learning possible) is similar to the one from the second, in that it builds on the same premises about learning—namely, that experience precedes understanding. At the same time, the third is distinct from the second in that it relies on more nuanced understanding of, and attention to, the process through which students acquire expertise. Thus, teaching from this third orientation draws on the goals and strategies associated with the first two models but requires an additional set of skills related to assessing students' knowledge and beliefs, knowing how people move from a novice to an expert level of understanding, and leading students toward new ways of thinking and knowing.[3]

Research studies in K–12 and postsecondary classrooms offer compelling evidence on the limitations of the "teaching as telling" model for teaching and learning. Yet that model continues to hold its own in the practice of and research on higher education; "teaching as telling" shapes the expectations of postsecondary students and faculty, the ways in which pedagogical practices are presented and carried out, and the typical strategies for evaluating college teaching.[4]

On arriving at LSCC, students, expecting the traditional model of college instruction, envisioned classrooms in which the professors dispensed their knowledge to students, largely through lectures. Significantly, students' expectations were largely confirmed by the organizational policies and structures of the college; and once inside particular classrooms, students understood teachers' spoken explanations as the crucial component of instruction. Consequently, in employing alternative pedagogical approaches, instructors like Lori and Beth challenged students' expectations and institutionally embedded norms simultaneously.

In this context, Lori's decision to adopt the roundtable format represented an obvious pedagogical transgression, and the resistance she faced from her students highlights the normally tacit understandings that students bring into postsecondary classrooms. In most of their classes students thought of learning as recording the information documented in textbooks and lectures and being able to repeat that information back to the instructor when they were tested. Furthermore, they expected professors to exert control over students. Hugh, for instance, delineated his criteria for good teaching through a comparison between his composition professor and his history professor. He described his composition instructor, Tim Dobbs, as exemplary—a professor with great knowledge of the subject and firm control over students' participation. Mr. Dobbs "catches me with his knowledge on things—he's got this great knowledge on things. Oh, yeah, everybody in the class should feel welcome to ask Mr. Dobbs a question—he'll explain it without opinion or anything, and he gives a lot of feedback with the papers."

In contrast, Hugh reported, his history instructor had not been dispensing enough information during her class. Moreover, he was disappointed with the amount of individual feedback he received on his written work. Expressing dissatisfaction with the overall result, Hugh concluded that his history professor needed to present more of her subject matter expertise to the class. "And maybe since we don't have very many assignments in the history class, and the few that we have, there's not really any feedback . . . I think that she could incorporate more of the knowledge that she has on history into the class." In Hugh's view, the history instructor did not present an adequate amount of information, especially by comparison with the authoritative Mr. Dobbs.

Hugh highlighted another problem with his history class, which he attributed to the instructor's lack of control over students in the classroom. In contrast to Mr. Dobbs' classroom, where students could feel "welcome" to "ask a question," in a process that would be orderly, efficient, and "informative," his history class, as Hugh described it, was poorly managed. He contended: "The typical class is like a high school class. There's a certain amount of class that's wasted, because there's just a kind of b.s.-ing. Or kids in the class are asking the kind of questions that would get the teacher off track—and things are just kind of going at a slow pace. It's not as strong as Mr. Dobbs's class." Because a number of students in his history class were also enrolled in the composition course, Hugh attributed the differences in classroom dynamics to the teacher and "the way that the teacher holds herself." Classroom control and the practice of professing were therefore integrally linked in Hugh's mind: an instructor who controlled students' behavior in an orderly classroom could demonstrate her professorial knowledge, thereby filling her role appropriately. Conversely, exercising "professorial" authority entailed controlling students' participation. In essence, the student's role is to accept and passively consume.

Another student, Melanie, noted the adverse effects of inade-

quate instruction on both current and future educational opportunities. "The professors need to fill you with enough basic
knowledge, or enough knowledge, so that when you go on to the
next course, you're not going to be totally out of the blue."

These underlying assumptions about knowledge and learning
not only structured students' expectations for the appropriate
instructional method (lecture and recitation) and course content
(facts to be tested), but also shaped their perspective on what
kinds of activities were relevant to *learning* the course material.
Nearly every student who voiced criticism of instructors' use of
classroom time, for instance, expressed frustration with "pointless" discussions. The activities that garnered criticism from the
vast majority of students were those which instructors had designed to explore students' own knowledge and to foster students' own analytical (meaning-making) capacities.

COMPOSITION 1A WITH LORI: ACTIVE RESISTANCE

From the start of the semester, Lori introduced activities intended
to create a space in which students could express their thoughts
and actively engage in reflection and inquiry. Her efforts corre-
sponded to the kind of "inquiry"-based approach to composition that the researcher George Hillocks rates highest with
respect to promoting students' learning.[5] Explaining her basic
philosophy, she asserted that students become engaged when
"they find things out for themselves." She viewed her instructional role in terms of harnessing their curiosity and providing
structures that would allow them to work with and learn from
one another.

Lori recognized that her teaching approach departed from the
traditional model of professing.

> Of course, I began teaching under the old system where the teacher
> is in control of the classroom; you are a lecturer, you go in there, and
> once you're done, you go on to something else. My stance is so dif-

ferent now—I even want to remove any authority, so to speak, and create a community.

In writing, I don't think that there can be an authoritative, "it has to be done this way" tradition. This is something about writing that I have been thinking about for a long, long time now. Yes, we do know that there are rules for grammar and rules for mechanics, and there are certain guidelines that you follow for different purposes. But as far as the quality of the information that goes in there—it has to do with convincing students that they really do have that information.

During this course, however, she encountered multiple layers of resistance from her students. Students challenged the policies documented in the syllabus, diverted substantial amounts of class time to what one student termed "niggling" procedural questions, and questioned her pedagogical approach. Fundamentally, the source of students' resistance lay in the conflict between their conceptions of college teaching and her pedagogical stance. The events that took place at the fourth class meeting served as a prelude to the discord that persisted for the rest of the semester, in which the classroom dynamics were dominated by an unusually resistant and resentful group of students.

"SHE IS NOT REALLY TEACHING US ANYTHING"

Class Session #4 (continued)

By the time Lori entered the classroom, the students were agitated. They began to bombard her with questions to gain clarification. Although Lori patiently addressed each question, after ten minutes of this spontaneous question-answer period, I realized that questions were exploding at a rising volume and had shifted from fairly neutral requests for direction to explicit challenges of Lori's syllabus. For example, Daniel asked, "Are all the comp classes being graded this way? I'm just trying to make sure that you're not being extra hard on us." Ian asked whether it would be okay to use alliteration, metaphors, and similes in this first assignment, then followed her response (sim-

*ply put, "It depends") with a confrontational assertion: "Well, that's
the way I write. I can do it that way if I want to."*
—Excerpt from field notes, Tuesday, September 10, 2002

That this vocal resistance erupted on the due date for the first
assignment suggests that it was provoked, in part, by students'
anxiety about the writing assignments. Between the third and
fourth class meetings, students had begun writing preliminary
drafts for the first essay and were experiencing varying levels of
confusion, anxiety, and doubt. As a result, some of them arrived
at the fourth session in search of concrete direction, specific
guidelines, and fundamental reassurance about their writing efforts. Instead, Lori deflected their efforts to elicit a standardized
template, by explaining that she could not offer simplistic rules
to govern every writing situation. She urged the students to take
on the authority for their own writing, to make decisions in the
context of their specific objectives for their own writing.

At the same time that students were experiencing anxiety
about their abilities to complete the writing assignments, Lori
continued to employ pedagogical strategies that violated students' expectations of college teaching. Midway through the
fourth class session, students appeared disgruntled and began
openly challenging Lori—hijacking the class to pursue their
questions and revealing the seeds of a distrust that would grow
throughout the semester.

In the end, what set the dynamics of this semester's class apart
was students' growing doubt about Lori's ability to teach. The
fierce resistance to Lori's class resulted from a convergence of
forces—including profound fears on the part of the students,
their interest in efficient and "useful" learning, and their assumptions about college instruction.

Ruth, the retired accountant, attributed her fellow students'
behavior to their youth and immaturity. Describing the conflict
as a power struggle between the vocal minority and Lori, she
explained that on some days, students would come to class

"ready to learn," but other times, they would do their best to divert the class from learning. As a result, "Sometimes the class would be totally excellent—it would be very informative. And then, the next class, maybe the students would think, 'Oh, well, we don't want all that learning today.'" On those days, the students persisted in "haggling" over the schedule, the requirements, and other details of the syllabus.

Ruth, who viewed herself as more mature and responsible than most of the students in the composition class, also understood her role as a student in different terms than her classmates did. Unlike the other students, Ruth was not attending college with the intention of earning a specific degree or advancing her career, but rather for the pleasure of continuing her education and pursuing new interests. Whereas others had enrolled in composition to fulfill an academic requirement, Ruth's motivation was entirely different. In the end, her assessment of the class was also substantially different from others'. She had enjoyed working on the assignments, and she was pleased with her efforts. When I asked her what she had learned from the course, she replied, "Basically, the big thing I really got out of it was more how to analyze what I read, think a little bit more deeply about what I'm reading, after I've read it, and what it meant to me, and things like that. I think that—I would read and you'd remember what you read, and you knew what this story's about, but you really didn't think [about] trying to look at it from the author's perspective of what he's really trying to put across, or . . . like a thesis."

Despite her different approach to learning in the composition course, Ruth shared her classmates' understanding of teaching as telling. She reported, for example, "I think it could be better, in the fact that . . . we've wasted a lot of valuable lesson time, you know." For Ruth, the classes that were best spent were the most informative sessions. When I asked her for examples of what she had termed "excellent, informative classes," she gave two examples. Both reflected the student consensus on good instruction: "I think the classes where, when she would actually put on the board, and go through—I'm trying to think—not too long ago—Oh, on cause and effect, when she actually took an example and wrote on the board about what would be the causes and the effects. . . . And I think that was really helpful." In other words, the most informative classes occurred when Lori presented information in lecture format, writing examples on the blackboard in order to illustrate her main lecture points. Ruth's second example of "excellent" teaching also defined teaching as the dispensation of data: "She gave us one excellent handout for the final test. . . . And it really was—she listed all the purposes, and she gave a lot of things that pertained to that particular purpose, and then on the next page were all the patterns and different criteria for them." In fact, Ruth found this handout so important that at the end of the semester she tried to make sure that other students still had the handout. "After I took it, I tried to pass that on to as many of the students as I could. And a lot of them, they didn't even have the paper." While this anecdote reinforces Ruth's perspective on these students' immaturity, it also illustrates her acceptance of the same paradigm of professorial authority that shaped other students' assessment of the class.

Lori's intent was to help students actively engage with texts, ideas, and hypotheses, rather than simply "giving out her knowledge" to individuals who would passively wait to be enlightened. Students, however, believed that by facilitating discussions, small-group activities, and other alternatives to the lecture format, Lori had failed to "inform" them adequately. Comparing her government professor with Lori, Maureen commented,

So I've been really impressed with [my government professor]. So she does relate on why this is important to the individual, and uses a lot of—tries to pull in a lot of examples. 'Now where have you seen this happen?' and she'll get a lot of feedback. Some of it's good, some of it's not, so she's very good at managing the students, too, so that nobody takes over and runs her class. So she's always in charge.

She's doing most of the talking; she gets a lot of feedback, but yet it's measured. Nobody can take over and speak for twenty minutes. You have a couple sentences, and then, she gets the reins again. So you don't ever have the feeling you're not part of it, but yet, you know that you're as much a part as everybody else is, and nobody else is running the show.

Maureen admired her government instructor's ability to present the course content and to illustrate its relevance to students' lives. In her view, the instructor's ability to convey the content was integrally related to strategies for "managing the students," and Maureen emphasized the nature of the control through a series of metaphors: "Nobody else is running the show," and students can contribute before the instructor "gets the reins again." In essence: student participation can easily take on a life of its own unless the professor carefully metes out short, structured opportunities for students to talk.

In his interview, Miguel expressed the same desire for more control in Lori's class.

> *Miguel:* This is my opinion. It's solely mine. She should take more initiative in controlling the class. She tends to get caught up into what the females in the class talk about, and it takes away from the time. A lot of times, she'll be up there writing, like, you know, how to compare and contrast, or writing examples and all that. And then, she's going to write up two more examples, but the time's out, yeah. A lot of that time was spent discussing—so far from wherever.
>
> *Becky:* All right, so what is the, what do you think has been the best, I mean the most productive class that you've taken, in terms of use of class time?
>
> *Miguel:* In terms of class time? Probably my math classes. Like, nobody does what they do in that [composition] class. Nobody blurts out stuff. Everybody's pretty quiet.

Miguel's comments about classroom control also imply criticism of the women in the class. True, during the last part of the semester, Lori's class consisted of more women than men (nine women and six men).[6] But the female students did not disproportionately dominate the group discussions in Lori's class, whether the comments are measured by frequency or by length. Miguel's emphasis on "what the females in the class talk about" may have reflected several related critiques: the amount of group discussion (as opposed to lecture), the amount and content of *female* discourse, and the free-form style of the discussion—at least when compared with math class, where "nobody blurts out stuff." The gender of the professorial authority figure is also an issue, and it is probably no coincidence that the math instructor, Miguel's model of professorial authority, is a man. Indeed, studies of university faculty suggest that women are constrained by gender-related constructions of authority; in several studies, students tended to rate women faculty higher when those women embodied traditional professorial authority, yet students rated them lower when the students perceived them as too authoritarian.[7] Thus, the acceptable range of professorial behavior was much more limited for women than men.

In the case of Lori, the instructional problem—as students perceived it—lay in her failure to control the class and institute a professorial pedagogy. And as a result, students considered Lori's expectations and instructions confusing. Suzanne, for instance, complained, "She says one thing and then she means a completely different, other thing." Likewise, Joy stated, "I don't know what to expect. She doesn't come out and say what she wants. She just figures that everything she wrote in that packet will do fine. And it's not the case. We need to know, really, what she specifically wants, because she's—I guess that comes back to the fact that she's unclear." Despite students' efforts to glean more specific instructions, Lori did not respond with a more controlling pedagogical approach. Her failure to demonstrate professorial expertise to students' satisfaction led first to resistance, then to distrust, as they began viewing Lori's requests and suggestions as unclear and arbitrary mandates.

THE CONSEQUENCES FOR LORI

The semester-long conflict in Lori's class was matched by several discouraging outcomes. By the end of semester, the attrition rate (approximately 50 percent) exceeded both the already high average across the department (35 percent) and the attrition rate across Lori's other comp courses (under 40 percent). Of the students that completed the course, few finished the requirements for earning an A or B; overall, 70 percent finished the semester with Cs. Whatever the actual learning outcomes for the students in the class, the low completion rate and students' tendency to fulfill only the minimum criteria for passing do not suggest great advances in learning. More significantly, the pervasive complaints from students in the class indicated that these dismal outcomes were integrally related to the pedagogical conflict. Ultimately, students' efforts to acquire useful information not only diverted the curriculum from what Lori had planned, but also failed to produce the kind of college instruction that the students expected. By the end of the semester, the most favorable assessment most students voiced about the experience was that they had passed the course and it was over.

Although the dynamics that emerged in Lori's classroom illustrate some of the problems of teaching, they were not the consequence of unskilled teaching. Instead, the conflict underscores the powerful effect of expectations on how students experience and assess their college encounters. Other studies have documented that students associate the traditional model of teaching with faculty competence and respond to alternative methods with skepticism or disrespect.[8] Indeed, professors who introduce alternative pedagogical practices can easily meet with resistance not just from students, but also from faculty colleagues and college administrators.[9]

Writing about his own efforts to introduce unconventional teaching practices, such as writing nonevaluative comments on student papers or revising the grading system, Tom Fox recognizes the strength of students' pedagogical conceptions. He found "a crucial problem" in his own classroom, he asserts: "the problem of students' histories of experience in the classroom. Just as students' experiences shape their understanding of their own roles as Students, their experiences also shape their conceptions of the role that teachers can take. . . . I find how little my intentions matter and how powerful are the influences of students' historical understandings of teachers."[10]

Students' historical understanding of teachers incorporates broader institutional definitions, beyond those of higher education and professorial authority. Indeed, assumptions about race, class, and gender entered into LSCC students' perceptions of teaching and learning.

Lori, one of the few African American instructors in the English department, experienced a form of culture shock in moving from the Eastside campus, where she had spent many years teaching classes with much higher proportions of African American and Latino students, to Far North Campus, where an underlying issue, possibly racially motivated, with her students throughout the semester was one of respect and courtesy. During my observations, a number of interactions during class sessions involved flippant remarks from students that seemed to teeter on the very edge of incivility.

Conceptions of professorial authority based on gender stereotypes presented another challenge for Lori (and the other women faculty members). Considering that women professors are at times expected to balance authority with an element of nurturing, it is not surprising that the role of professor seemed much more complicated for Lori and Beth than for any of the male professors I observed.

COMPOSITION 1A WITH BETH: PASSIVE RESISTANCE

Like Lori, Beth explicitly defined the learning objectives of her course in abstract terms. She used the writing process as a springboard for reflective inquiry: thinking through ideas, answering questions, and constructing arguments. Also like Lori, Beth sought to develop students' abilities to think and write critically, through a set of carefully designed activities intended to increase students' own authority as writers. In her first interview, Beth told me, "My goals are all thinking goals. I really think that writing is thinking, largely." She described her instructional role as one of designing opportunities for students to engage in conversation, "make meaning of language," and understand how to "take part in the larger current of social debate."

Beth's weekly class schedule incorporated ten minutes of journal writing, often with prompts related to the day's reading assignment; discussion of the reading assignment; short lectures on aspects of the writing process, individual or group exercises targeted at the day's topic; and peer review exercises.

Of these activities, students made positive comments about the journal writing and the lectures. Discussions and peer review, by contrast, were not well received. Only two students in the entire class exhibited interest in discussing the assigned readings. Kyra was one of the two who offered well-elaborated responses, volunteered answers, and posed analytical questions of her own. It was clear to Kyra, however, that other students were not interested in the analytical discussions that Beth tried to facilitate. Kyra remarked, "I was surprised with the [low] level of participation within the class. I think a lot of the students in there weren't really taking things very seriously, which kind of annoyed me a lot of the time, where I really wanted to discuss specifics of a particular essay, and really get involved in that essay." Not coincidentally, Kyra was also the only student who did not advocate a more controlled form of group discussion. "Beth gives people the chance to articulate themselves—when there's something I want to speak about, then I speak. And when you offer that freedom in class, then sometimes you have to give up something, and sometimes what you give up is a control thing." Instead, Kyra expressed vexation with the majority of her classmates and dismay at what she described as their inability to take the work seriously. She noted that other students contributed interesting ideas, but that few were willing to engage with the essays—an attitude that she attributed to immaturity. So although she was disappointed with the quality of the group discussions, she enjoyed the opportunity to speak freely and appreciated Beth's ability to give up some of that "control thing."

"IT'S OKAY TO MISS CLASS, SINCE WE DON'T REALLY DO ANYTHING"

Representing the more typical view of discussion, Sarah remarked, "Sometimes our conversations in class are a little too long, and all that is because people like to go on and on and on and on. So it drags it all out. . . . The biggest problem in our English class is when she would ask about the stories—that's mostly when a lot of people would get into an in-depth conversation. And it's like, a simple question." I verified that when Sarah spoke of "the stories," she was referring to the short nonfiction essays that Beth assigned for every class. Sarah's comments suggested that she perceived the discussions more as recitations, during which Beth asked questions that called for short replies. During the same interview, Sarah also admitted that she had never really enjoyed reading "stories." For her, each assigned text was simply a boring task. If something informative could be said about the text, it would be Beth who expressed it.

Throughout the semester I observed this resistance to analyzing the readings. During each session, Beth employed a variety of techniques to facilitate discussion; for example, she used the journal prompts as the starting point for discussion, thus enabling students to contribute thoughts they had just been writing about. She tried to find ways to connect the themes to students' personal experience. She asked students to comment on their initial reactions, whether intellectual, emotional, or visceral. Often this approach elicited such feedback as, "Well, it wasn't as bad as the LAST thing we read," or a facile response aimed at the author such as, "Who cares?" (Liz) or "Stop whining" (Jake).

During that week that Beth had juxtaposed several essays on gender in the readings, students almost immediately shut down the conversation with statements about the futility of analyzing gender issues at all. Jack opined, "Men and women are just different. It's like comparing apples and oranges." Stu followed up with "Sometimes things can be simple. They don't always have to be complex."

The content of these essays, pointed arguments about gender relations and the social order, led students to read them as "stories" or creative expressions of each author's opinion. Consequently, they viewed each text as a set of beliefs that they might react to—but to what end? Beth had imagined interrogating the underlying assumptions about gender, deconstructing the arguments, and demonstrating each author's rhetorical strategies. The students, however, saw no reason to spend time on the various authors' opinions. Indeed, Beth reported to me that some students wrote constant complaints in their journals about the reading assignments, assessing the topics as really, really boring. Beth was stymied by students' responses. At the end of the semester, she reported:

> It was just so frustrating that—they really seemed to hate the readings in that class. . . . Liz, in her journal, said that she hated the readings: they were just boring and horrible.
> And so if the readings are what I've got to try and foster critical discussions, and they don't want to engage with the readings—they're bored by them—then . . .
> I tried to ask questions to draw out an interesting discussion, based on the readings. The students just have to be willing to work with me a little bit, and those guys in there just weren't. I had this vision of building more and more engagement with the text and to their assignments, but it fell apart. . . . The readings were the mechanism, but they weren't working.

As in Lori's class, the majority of students in Beth's were unwilling to engage in analyses of the readings and uninterested in doing so. Stacey was the student who provided the starkest as-

sessment of Beth's failed efforts to facilitate discussion, engagement with the texts, and other collaborative learning experiences. In reference to Beth's class, Stacey simply stated, "It's okay
to miss class, since we don't really do anything."

While few students agreed with Stacey about not doing *anything* in Beth's composition class, many shared her lack of regard
for the peer review component of the course. Even Kyra, whose
preference for a more robust and student-led discussion of the
readings was atypical, criticized the activity. In Kyra's words,
"In these peer groups that we had, the students didn't know
what they were looking for in the first place, so it was just not
very helpful, because they're not getting any feedback from their
peers, who really don't know anything anyway." Jenn also sin-
gled out the peer review process as an example of a worthless
activity, "because you're having other people who are around
your age and basically have as bad, or worse writing as you do,
or really don't want to stay [in class], and just basically scrib-
ble all over your paper. I mean, I'd rather have somebody who
knows what the hell they're talking about grade my paper, than
somebody who is just going to sit there and say, 'Yeah, it's okay.'"
Reiterating Jenn's point, Liz also contended that her peers did
not have the expert knowledge required to assess her paper cor-
rectly. "I don't want some stupid kid grading my paper. For all I
know, the kid next to me could be some kid that makes all Fs in
school. I mean, you just pass your paper to the kid next to you,
and he reads it, and he goes, 'Oh, that's good,' and he passes it
back to you. It's not productive at all, it's a waste of time, if anything."

None of these students seemed to understand the task as Beth
intended, nor as she had originally presented it to the class. The
peer review was not meant to involve "grading" each other's papers. In fact, Beth had distributed a rubric for looking at each
other's work and explicitly stated the goals of peer review during
several class sessions.[11] Students' most frequent objections to the
activity stemmed from the importance they attached to the grad-

ing process, as well as their understanding that the professor is the only one with the expert knowledge required to accurately correct and evaluate their work. As a student in another section remarked, "I really hate the whole fact that sometimes university professors will have TAs in their auditoriums. And they allow those TAs to grade students. You know what? I didn't come to college for some student working towards their degree to grade me. You're the professor. I want your expert opinion."

By the second half of the semester, students refused to participate in the peer review activity at all. On one occasion, students assembled in their peer review groups, but did not exchange papers with others. The next time peer review appeared on the schedule, Beth polled students at the start of the class session, asking, "How many of you brought drafts for peer review?" Two students raised their hands, but later, when Beth directed everyone to meet in their groups, those two students were the first to leave the classroom, having neither shared their drafts nor even interacted with their groups. During the end-of-semester interviews, I asked students why they did not prepare drafts for peer review. Liz, Ryan, and Serena explained: they had written drafts and brought them to class; however, they had no intention of participating in peer review but simply submitted their drafts to Beth at the end of class. These students were fully prepared for class; they simply refused to share drafts with their peers.

In retrospect, I believe that two other issues were at work in the peer review exercise. First, the fear of exposing their inadequacies to peers played a role in some students' reluctance to participate. Serena was one student in Beth's class who mentioned her hesitance to expose herself to peer evaluators. She said, "I don't like other people reading my stories and stuff. I want to care about what I write, so when we had to do that, I didn't bring anything with me. Because I just have this thing— that if they read my stuff, they're going to think I'm stupid or something, and that I don't know how to write."

A second issue related to the grading system, which did not

include any points for the peer review exercises. Given the importance of an instructor's grading approach in signaling what matters to students, Beth's students may have understood the lack of grading as an indication that less importance was assigned to the activity. As a result, students were able to treat peer review as an optional activity without fear that their lack of participation would detract from their final grades.

THE CONSEQUENCES FOR BETH

Like Lori, Beth faced some resistance from her students. In the end, however, the dynamics in Beth's case differed from those in Lori's. By refusing to participate altogether, students positioned themselves as more passive participants, and in effect, forced Beth into the role of expert and explainer. Students did not lose trust in Beth's authority, and by the end of the semester, students spoke admiringly of Beth's knowledge and skill in teaching writing. Although Beth had hoped to accomplish more, the end-of-semester outcomes were encouraging; the students who enrolled in Beth's class tended to complete the course, and a majority of those completers exceeded the minimum requirements for a C. Furthermore, as will be seen in Chapter 6, students evaluated their semester with Beth overall as a successful learning experience with a professor who "really relates."

In each of these classrooms, the teacher tried to foster authorial capabilities of her students, by asking them to engage with and produce texts, rather than merely passively consume and transcribe information. In their efforts to support students' authority, Beth and Lori both designed a semester of classroom activities that brought small groups of students together to share their expertise with each other. Each instructor carefully guided students' interactions—from selecting particular students to work with each other to providing a series of tasks over the course of the semester that were intended to foster students' skills and confidence in writing and analysis.

The objectives of these activities were totally lost on students. Students' dislike of these activities and resistance to them reflected the desire for instructors to transmit the course content clearly and efficiently. Students therefore exhibited both anger and frustration over activities they perceived as unworthy for college-level instruction. This attitude proved to be a problem for Lori and Beth, who had essentially designed their Comp 1A courses around such activities. In the case of both teachers, students put up resistance to the course design.

Unfortunately, the stranglehold of the professorial paradigm on higher education also presents a tremendous obstacle to the development of any real insight into the problems that postsecondary teaching and learning confront—to understanding that these problems are attributable to more than inadequate teaching techniques, underprepared students, or weak course content. In the end, none of these explanations adequately accounts for the student resistance or end-of-semester outcomes in Lori's and Beth's composition classes.

CHAPTER 6

PROFESSORS WHO "COME DOWN TO OUR LEVEL"

EVEN BEFORE STUDENTS step into the composition classroom, their varying levels of interest in the subject, their assumptions about college instruction, and their uncertainties create a series of instructional dilemmas. Further complicating the picture are professors' conceptions of what constitutes appropriate college student behavior, and teachers' lack of understanding about what prevents students from acting in accordance with those norms. At the same time, when instructors recognize the reasons for students' disappointing performance—whether in class or on assignments—they are much more likely to respond effectively. By virtue of their professorial authority, instructors have a tremendous influence on students' sense of competence and willingness to seek help. An instructor's ability to assuage students' fears can be the first and most important step toward actively inviting students into the classroom to accomplish what they perceived as challenging but "doable" work.

This chapter presents the instructional perspectives and strategies of two particularly skilled composition instructors at Lake Shore Community College—both of whom have demonstrated success in helping students meet the standards of first-semester composition at the college. Focusing on these two instructors,

Beth and Julie, in this chapter I discuss the approach that proved most successful in helping students pass composition. To state it briefly, these instructors expected rigorous work from students, provided both the subject matter content and explicit instructions for approaching each assignment, and convinced students that they had the ability to accomplish the work. It seems a matter of common sense that such strategies would yield positive results, but without the teachers' understanding and addressing the issues outlined in previous chapters, simply applying these strategies would not produce the same results.

In many ways, Beth and Julie were no different from their colleagues in the English department at Lake Shore Community College. Like the other composition instructors I observed, they provided detailed, explicit instruction. The instructors all agreed that the students enrolled in Comp 1A were academically capable not only of passing the course, but of succeeding. Teachers' confidence in students' abilities is critical; research studies suggest that such optimism may be the most fundamental of the factors affecting an instructor's success with less advantaged students.[1]

Moreover, all of the professors in this study described their commitment to teaching community college students as opposed to students at a four-year college. Across the two-year colleges I have visited, instructors have, at times, made references to "four-year wannabes," faculty members they perceive to be working at the two-year level only because they were unable to find employment at four-year colleges. Such comments presuppose two categories of professors—those who sincerely enjoy working with two-year college students, and those who have "settled" on this path, in order to remain in higher education. In my study, several spoke of the rewards of working with students generally deemed underprepared. Here is one fairly typical statement: "In an environment like this, some of the students don't have a command of the King's English and many of them have no idea what college is all about but, *man!* they've got some amazing life experiences and viewpoints on things, and it's just a matter of their learning how to put that out in a formal essay."

Through their written feedback to students and during teacher-student conferences, I witnessed the respect and appreciation instructors felt for students' writing.[2] Their comments consistently highlighted the positive features of each student's essay: elements of the writer's style, organizational strategy, and ideas. The instructors' subtle readings illuminated aspects of students' texts that would otherwise have escaped my notice, such as literary flourishes and the intriguing seeds of thought that lay below the prosaic surface. In addition, instructors spoke thoughtfully about their pedagogical philosophies and the kinds of changes they planned to adopt to improve the course and, in turn, students' learning. Optimistic, reflective practitioners, these instructors spent immense time and energy on behalf of their students. And yet despite all the instructors' commitment and hard work, the completion rate varied widely across different sections of Comp 1A: it ranged from 45 percent to 80 percent, with an average rate only slightly higher than the department-wide rate of 60 percent.[3]

The variation in completion rates cannot be attributed to major differences in student abilities or in the course curricula across composition sections. By collegewide policy, enrollment in Comp 1A is limited to students who receive an adequate score on the college's literacy assessment test. Thus, the students who enroll in the course have been judged academically prepared for the course by the college's own assessment policies. Furthermore, the instructors all follow the guidelines and assignment structure of a standardized syllabus, which minimizes curricular variation across composition classrooms.

Regardless of the rate of attrition, the pattern of student participation and withdrawal in Comp 1A was the same from classroom to classroom. Most students who failed or withdrew from the course had gotten stuck on writing assignments at the beginning of the course and either completed none of the required essays or managed to complete only the first essay.

Beth's and Julie's courses were distinctive in that a higher proportion of students submitted the first essay assignment, completed the second assignment, and eventually finished the course with a passing grade. By the end of the semester, not only had a higher percentage of students persisted in Beth's and Julie's classrooms, but those students also described Beth and Julie differently than they did other instructors—not simply with the respect and appreciation accorded most professors, but with adulation.

In fact, the crucial dimension of both Beth's and Julie's approaches hinged on students' perceptions. It was not the classroom dynamics per se that mattered, as much as *students' perceptions* of the classroom dynamics. Beth's and Julie's success with their composition students had three related dimensions. First, seeing that their instructor possessed expert knowledge and the ability to explain it, students trusted these professors' subject matter mastery. Second, Beth and Julie epitomized a form of authority based on interpersonal relations, which students perceived as more confidence-inspiring than traditional professing.[4] Third, these professors expected rigorous work from students; they also provided enough explicit instruction (from the student point of view) about approaching each assignment. As a whole, this pedagogical approach persuaded students that they were more than capable of accomplishing the work.

Convincing students that they will succeed at college-level work is difficult, particularly because professors' expertise can be immensely intimidating to students. As Colleen explained (in Chapter 2), the professors who inspire the most fear are those to whom she would, if she could gather enough courage, give this advice: "Come down to our level a little bit. I know you have a lot of stuff to teach us, but don't be so high on that pedestal that we can't reach you." Feeling intimidated can easily lead to distancing and disengagement in any classroom; in college classrooms where taking initiative is the mark of a "serious" or "motivated" student, students might feel highly motivated to learn without acting in a way that conveys that seriousness to the instructor. This proves even more problematic in composition classrooms where professors, hoping that students will assume the voice of authority in their writing, do not want to tell students what to write. As I argue in the previous chapter in the context of Lori's class, students trusted instructors who clearly demonstrated their subject matter knowledge; thus, Beth and Julie's authority depended on their first demonstrating professorial expertise.

Colleen's interview comments provide the clearest illustration of the consequences of this paradox for the professor. After remarking on what she perceived as her philosophy professor's arrogant demeanor, Colleen explained that she feared the teacher would consider her stupid if she asked him any questions (see Chapter 2). Another student, generalizing about his classmates, asserted that some students are simply intimidated because their professors assign grades. Such students, he contended, "don't want to look like a fool" (Chapter 4). The features that distinguished Beth and Julie's teaching from that of other highly competent and admired professors came through in students' descriptions: students emphasized Beth and Julie's ability to "come down to" students' level and to "relate." The instructional success of these teachers depended first and foremost on their actively encouraging students and assuaging their most debilitating fears.

"COMING DOWN" TO STUDENTS' LEVEL

The analyses in previous chapters indicate that because students are interested in acquiring content knowledge, the presence of "informative" course content is crucial to college teaching and learning in their eyes. Although students saw the traditional au-

Professors who relate	Excellent professors
"My composition professor really cares, and she relates. And she tries to help, everywhere she can."	"It seems like he's pretty intelligent; I think he's a pretty good teacher altogether and, you know, everything he's teaching is pretty much right."
"He's really good at saying like, 'No, that's not right,' without putting anyone down. . . . If there were any questions that I wanted to ask, I don't think I would hesitate to go up and ask him."	"If you notice when he's talking, he is so smart. He knows so many things and you're just like, 'Wow.' Like, I remember about my second week when I got in there, I was like, 'Golly. How can you know so much stuff?'"
"I like her because she gets personal with you. She'll ask things about you, about your life, like with that form that we filled out: What you were doing in college, why were you there, what made you come, things like that. It's a little bit more personal than what my other teachers did. Besides my speech teacher, she's really the only teacher that even cared to get to know the students personally."	"I think that he's an excellent teacher. I think he is so thorough in his material—like, a lot of questions that might have been asked don't need to be. . . . I would take him again. I think he requires a lot out of his students."

Table 6.1

thoritative professor who explains the content as the most legitimate model, Beth and Julie, the professors who "related," minimized the distance between their students and themselves, in part by understanding how students perceived the course content and by recognizing and responding to students' lack of confidence. A crucial piece of the two women's pedagogy consisted of their efforts to understand how students were interacting with the course content—both cognitively and emotionally—and to respond accordingly. Beth and Julie were thereby able to close the gap between their students and the course content, while encouraging those students to persist.

When students attributed their persistence and success to professors, the ability of those teachers to relate or come down to students' level was at the heart of their account. In contrast, when they spoke of other excellent professors, they focused on the traditional dimension of subject matter expertise. A few representative descriptions illustrate this basic difference.

In the case of Beth, students consistently alluded to her accessibility. Serena highlighted Beth's friendliness, saying, "She seems real friendly. Like some professors will be like, 'Oh, I'll be in my office,' but you're real hesitant to go to them, because of the way they are. But she seems like she wouldn't mind if you went to go ask her questions and stuff." For Serena, "the way they are" does not include demeaning or belittling behavior; to the contrary, she describes the typical professor as both knowledgeable and helpful. But Serena admits here that even when professors offer extra help during their office hours, she remains hesitant about seeking their assistance.

Serena also observed, "She's like a teacher who is not that educated, like compared to our other teachers," and Ryan added, "She brings herself kind of down to our level." To both of them (and to their classmates), Beth appeared more open and friendly than the typical professor at LSCC. Again, other professors had not acted *unfriendly*, but Beth had made a conscious effort to meet students at their "level."

In this way, Beth, with a Ph.D. in English, commanded respect for her subject matter expertise and her ability to explain it to students, but not in a "high and mighty" way. By embodying these key aspects of college teaching (professing), Beth earned her students' trust in her competence. At the same time, she did not remain in the distant (and distanced) position of the stereotypical professor, many levels above students. In Serena's terms, Beth comes across to students as highly educated, but much less threatening than a typical professor.

Similarly, Julie's students spoke in glowing terms about how she encouraged them not to give up when faced with challenging work. Colleen said, "When we did the research paper, that scared the hell out of me. I was freaking out. Julie could tell just by looking at me. She's like, 'You'll do fine. Calm down.' She encouraged me like nobody has ever encouraged me. I made a very direct point to get her again next semester."

Furthermore, Colleen attributed her persistence in her philosophy course to Julie's support. "Because of the way Julie encourages us, it will make a lot more students come back, where they won't be scared off. Like my philosophy and history classes: if I hadn't had Julie in my corner, I probably would have dropped most of my classes. They need more teachers like her, ones that encourage the student to try harder and give them better examples on how to go about getting things accomplished, instead of browbeating and scaring them."

Meeting students at "their level" did not mean that Beth and Julie diluted the course content or decreased their demands on students, for in the expectations for students' class preparation and for the quality of students' written work, both instructors maintained a level of rigor that was at least as high as that of other composition instructors. Rather, when students described these professors' ability to "come down to our level," they were speaking of the teachers' friendliness, accessibility, and approachability. These instructors may have made the coursework easier to understand, but it was not unchallenging.

The Comp 1A assignments on the standard syllabus appeared challenging and time-consuming to composition students, regardless of their instructor. But from the start of the semester, both Beth and Julie indicated that in addition to submitting the core paper assignments (and revisions), students would also be responsible for completing reading assignments before every class meeting. Moreover, by requiring students to respond to the assigned reading and "counting" students' comments, they held students responsible for that work. In addition to facilitating discussions of the reading assignments, for example, Julie often asked that students contribute at least one comment on the reading assignment, which she then counted as students' attendance for the day. Both Beth and Julie incorporated questions about the reading into journal prompts, to which students responded during class and which they submitted as one of the required journal assignments. In these ways, Beth and Julie followed through on the expectations for student participation set out in their respective syllabi. Beth, for one, had noted in her syllabus that students should "prepare to engage in conversation." She contended, "The class will be greatly enriched if all of our voices are heard." Similarly, Julie had explained in her syllabus that she hoped to "engage" students during class and that she would expect their preparation for and participation in various classroom activities. In both cases, these expectations implied that students could and would contribute to the curriculum used throughout the semester. This approach served two functions. First, these professors indicated from day one of the course that students had both the *responsibility* and the *capacity* to contribute to the class. Second, this approach fostered a mutual relationship based on responsibility. Julie explained in her syllabus, "By enrolling in my course, you and I are entering into a contract whereby you agree to the following stipulations." Following her list of stipulations (such as active participation in class discussions and group work), she explained how she would reciprocate: "What you can expect from me is fairness in grading and a sincere desire to help those students who honestly want to improve their writing, critical thinking, and research skills." On the very first day of class, Julie further clarified that her typical standard for assignments submitted would be A- or B-level work. In other words, she clarified that she would expect more than minimal work.

Another crucial dimension of Beth's and Julie's instructional approaches was these teachers' ability to provide enough detailed, explicit instruction that students could attempt each assignment without being crippled by confusion and insecurity.

Indeed, students' self-doubts severely limited their tolerance for confusing or unfamiliar activities and assignments—reflecting the typical attitude of "risk-averse" students. As a result, frustration with the level of difficulty of the coursework or confusion over the instructors' expectations about graded assignments could quickly push students to the point of quitting.

In discussing the help they had received from Beth or Julie, students consistently mentioned the importance of clear instructions at the outset of the assignment, and of detailed explanations of the instructor's comments during revision and editing. Eva, for example, who benefited from Julie's instructions for each assignment, emphasized their role in reducing her anxiety: "And she would give us the outline, like the sheet where she'd say what she wanted in the paragraphs. So, that would help a lot too. She was very clear on what she wanted us to do."

As for feedback on students' drafts, Beth marked students' papers, then audiotaped more detailed comments, which she returned with students' written drafts. Sarah, one of many students who appreciated this method, explained the advantages:

> Beth will tell you what you've done—because she pretty much reads the paper with you, on the tape. I should have brought my tape and let you listen to it. But you have the paper in front of you, and she goes error by error, what you've done wrong, and explains to you why it's wrong.
>
> I never had a teacher do that before. You know, it was kind of like, "Well, you did this, this, and this wrong. Why is it wrong? Well, you need to look that up."

During an interview, Julie described the importance of providing well-elaborated instructions to students, especially for the students she teaches at the Eastside campus, a site with a much higher percentage of nontraditional students.

> I think I've said this already: I'm a little bit more detailed in the kind of directions that I give now than I was even five years ago. In the past, I was kind of just thinking, "Well, I'm the teacher and you're

the student. You should understand what I want you to do. I mean, what do you mean you need more specific directions?" Now it's more like, "Think about them, Julie. If you were in their shoes, what would you want? Oh, okay, yeah, this is what I want. I want specific directions." So I find that I give them more specific directions now.

Linda, one of the students in Julie's class that semester, and someone who had attempted the Comp 1A course multiple times, offered her opinion about what helps keep a student in the class. Like Julie, Linda spoke of the instructor's ability to put herself in her students' shoes. "You know what I think it is? I think it's the instructors. Julie is really cool, and I'm not just saying that—I mean, I've taken a lot of different writing courses, and I never had the same instructor. But it's always the way *they* see it. They don't look at the way the student is seeing it. I mean, they say, 'Well, now, you do it this way.' But, why am *I* wrong and why are *you* right?"

Maintaining high expectations and offering clear and consistent instructions, however, worked only when students perceived themselves as able to meet the standards and follow the directions. The huge influence that professors exercise over students' feelings of efficacy is the key here. Professors who underestimated the level of students' anxiety tended unintentionally to exacerbate those fears.

Furthermore, individuals who feel like outsiders to the college environment may require a greater level of support to persist. Both Beth and Julie understood this—and acted accordingly. At the start of the semester, Beth told me, she tries to assess students' attitudes toward the class, asking students for written responses to a few introductory questions. The short survey includes a question about students' past experiences with English, and Beth told me later that there are "probably about 10 or 20 percent every semester that just talk about how demoralizing it was, and how their writing is so terrible." As a result, she tries to be sensitive to students' fears when mapping out the details of the course. For the students who appear to be struggling the most, she tries to provide extra one-on-one assistance, without appearing to single them out as less competent members of the class. "And then," she added, "I just do the same thing with them that I do with all the other students, in terms of trying to just make them feel comfortable in the class and feel like their contributions are being heard and valued, and give them constant encouragement in their journals—that kind of thing. I think they just take a little bit more of that. They need a little bit more of that affirmation, to give them confidence to keep going."

Similarly, Julie spoke of the importance of encouraging students and helping them to persist in the class:

> Quite honestly, the majority of the time when students become better writers, it's because all of a sudden they believe, Hey, I can do this. Whereas before, they walked in going, "I'm not a good writer," so they're already predestined: "Oh, I'm not going to do well." And I tell them, "You need to just get all those thoughts out of your head, because you will do well. And you will pass the class. And you will do what I say."
>
> And so that's what it boils down to. So it's just all in their heads. And so I usually have to motivate and constantly stroke their back saying, "You can do it. You will do it. Don't panic," and then that usually gets them through.
>
> So giving students that kind of reinforcement, I think that's the biggest thing before anything else—before teaching research skills, before teaching the thesis statement. All that, quite honestly, if I can convince them that they can do it, then they will: regardless of what I asked them to do, they will do it.
>
> So that's really what I found I have to make sure that I'm doing in the classroom as a whole. To the whole class, "You will do it. You will, I promise." And then, individually, consistently individually, you know, "You are doing well. You are progressing. You will make it." So that, to me, is the biggest thing.

According to each of the students in their respective classes, Beth and Julie provided enough positive feedback to convince students to persist and try harder.

> Another thing I like about her feedback is that she has a lot of positive feedback, even if you go in there thinking: "This paper, this is just something I wrote. I don't think she's going to like it." But she gives positive feedback, and that gives me more inspiration, like, "I thought it was bad, but she thinks it's okay." So I like that—that she's not negative. (Diego, regarding Julie's comments)

> The best thing about Julie is the way she critiques your papers. The way she puts her comments on there. "Wow." "Great job." "Awesome paper." "I knew you could do it." "You finally got it." All these little comments encourage you like you would never believe. (Colleen)

Such encouragement minimizes the sting of making mistakes and being corrected (which is how students seemed to understand most comments from instructors). Over and over, students in Beth's and Julie's classes referred to their typical responses to instructors' feedback as feeling "belittled," overwhelmed, and demoralized.

> Also, she doesn't tell you this in person. She'll let you read it. And I think that's awesome, too, because you don't have to stand there and feel belittled, if you make a mistake or something. You can get home and read this paper and go, "Wow, she really liked my paper. This is so cool." Or if you see something negative on there, it's okay. (Colleen, describing Julie)

> I'm glad that she doesn't write comments in red, because when you see a lot of red, the first thing you think is "Oh, my goodness." But then I read her comments: "It has potential and it's wonderful, and I think if you focus, it will be a little bit better." (Charmaine, describing Julie)

> I mean, she's easy to feel comfortable with, because she's not a "That's wrong, that's wrong" type of person. She can take something

wrong and turn it into a positive thing to keep you motivated, and work with you. And I think that's motivating, instead of saying, "That's wrong—we don't do it that way," she'll say, "Well, that way is good, but I think this way will be a lot better." (Sarah, describing Beth)

ACADEMIC VALIDATION AND STUDENT SUCCESS

Beth and Julie filled the role of the authoritative expert in their classrooms, in line with the traditional model of postsecondary instruction; however, they also engaged in strategies aimed at alleviating students' anxieties and provided students with constant encouragement. In each case, the instructor recognized the potential for the fear students were feeling to impede their success. Students' appreciation of Beth and Julie's encouragement echoes Laura Rendon's 1994 research on Latino students at four-year colleges. In Rendon's work, the students who persisted attributed their success to being actively invited (even pulled in) to college by key adults—counselors, instructors, or other adults in the academic sphere. "What had transformed nontraditional students into powerful learners and persisters were incidents in which some individual, either inside or outside class, had validated them. . . . Validating agents took an active interest in students. They provided encouragement for students and affirmed them as being capable of doing academic work and supported them in their academic endeavors and social adjustment."[5] Studies of underrepresented students in math and science programs also point to the importance of validation, reiterating that students who feel like outsiders (in this case, in the "culture of science") need more than the *opportunity* to become involved. Such students benefit greatly from interactions that affirm their academic competence and ability to succeed. As Moreno and Muller report in their discussion of first-year calculus, "Direct contact with a faculty member through which their ability as a mathematician or scientist is validated increases the likelihood that African Americans, Latinos, and women will stay in a quantitative major."[6]

In employing strategies for minimizing fear, both Beth and Julie narrowed the distance between themselves and their students. By the end of the semester, students in these two classes tended to attribute their success in passing Composition 1A to the supportive relationship developed with the instructor. Significantly, when students discussed their accomplishments in the course, their newly acquired confidence was at the top of the list.

In the case of Comp 1A at LSCC, a mechanism for developing the teacher-student relationship is built into the structure of the course: in the process of submitting drafts and making revisions, students engage in one-on-one conversations with their instructor, who offers positive comments, suggestions for change, and feedback on students' ideas. This relationship depended, however, on students' taking the first step to submit a draft. So when a student like Mara spoke of her instructor's encouragement, she gave this example: "Like, on one paper, he wrote, 'If you have any trouble . . .' or 'If you're having any questions,' or something, 'come contact me.' And that was really important." This offer was possible, though, only because Mara had submitted her essays and continued attending the class. Students who did not submit that first graded assignment did not benefit from this kind of interaction.

In this regard, a crucial strategy that both Julie and Beth applied at the start of each semester was to ask students to participate in low-stakes writing exercises during class sessions. This enabled the instructors to provide some positive feedback on students' ideas and writing before the first essay was due. Both instructors, for example, required in-class writing about the reading, in the form of "journal entries" or informal "free writes," to which the teachers responded in writing, with informal conversational remarks. Thus began a one-on-one relationship between professor and student around the students' ideas. In both cases, this journal writing "counted" in the grading scheme for the class, but points were awarded simply for submitting some writing, thereby minimizing anxiety on the part of students about the quality of their work.

From the start of the semester, Beth and Julie also actively reached out to students, establishing encouraging relationships and fostering a comfortable classroom atmosphere. In some instances, they engaged in practices that are not standard in postsecondary contexts, such as calling students who missed class, or sending spontaneous e-mails to individual students from week to week. An interesting result of these strategies was that students were much less likely simply to disappear from the class without letting the instructor know. Most of the time, when students considered withdrawing from Julie's or Beth's classes, they spoke to their instructor about it directly, rather than simply slipping out of class and filling out the paperwork. By the end of the semester, both instructors were able to pinpoint specific, well-elaborated reasons for students' inability to complete the course, information that highlighted the bonds they had established with students since the beginning of the semester.

The dominant view of student success in the four-year college context suggests that student engagement or involvement during the first year of college is a determining factor in the rate of persistence. Furthermore, a student's level of involvement is often framed as a matter of individual choice, but that viewpoint overlooks contextual or situational factors that complicate students' transition to college.[7]

The view from inside these classrooms offered evidence that complications in students' lives outside school played a considerable role in attrition. "Life is what happened to these people" was Julie's summary of the attrition in her classroom that semester. Similarly, another instructor attributed the high attrition rate across the department to students' overlapping responsibilities and work schedules. Describing his concern over student attrition, he mused,

> I can say, "Well, they have things going on in their lives. They're just not doing the work." And then, on the other hand, I always feel

guilty about it. I always feel responsible for it, at least to a degree. I always think or always ask myself, "What could I have done or said to make it different?" or "What part have I played in their inability to turn in papers?"

You know, they're getting a clear assignment sheet each time, they're getting sample papers, we have discussion. I make very thorough comments on their papers, more than most people probably do. So I'm thinking, "Give them plenty of guidance for the paper that they've gotten in, plus future papers they might turn in." And they still don't succeed.

At the end of the semester, when he spoke of the low completion rate for his class (under 50 percent), he described the dropout rate primarily as a result of students' simply not handing in papers. At the same time, he voiced a sense of helplessness. In truth, community college students, like many college students at every level of higher education, maintain complicated configurations of school, work, and family responsibilities. And yet, he wondered, was there something else he could do as an instructor? He told me that every semester he inspects the withdrawal slips on which students mark specific reasons for dropping the course, hoping for clues to how to address students' noncompletion. As he explained, "There's a reason code in the withdrawal slip. If they drop themselves, they identify the reason why, which is an interesting clue. And in my experience, about half of them say, 'Conflict between school and work.' But there are all sorts of things. 'Class was too hard for me.' They don't normally say, 'The teacher wasn't as good as I'd hoped.' But they'll say, 'Personal problems,' or 'Health.' Transportation problems are an often-cited reason. So those reason codes for those who drop themselves are somewhat revealing, but not very." He, like many of his colleagues, has consistently made modifications to his courses, in hopes that the completion rate will also improve. But in the end he remains uncertain what conditions in the classroom, if any, might increase students' chances of success.

This instructor viewed the high attrition rate in composition as inevitable when students were maintaining overlapping responsibilities and work schedules. He did not, however, identify the fear factor. And although completing Comp 1A was essentially about writing the papers, the fear and confusion that were driving students to quit cannot be overestimated. If we look at Beth's and Julie's classes, it becomes clear that strategies intended to minimize fear helped make the class less difficult for students. Linda, the self-acknowledged expert on dropping Comp 1A, explained why she had withdrawn so many times: "The reason I would drop would be if I couldn't figure out what was going on, and how things should be done." When I asked her what advice she had for future composition students, she simply said, "Just do the papers—just do it. Don't give up. I think that's what happens to most of the students. It's too much: they just give up."

And because many of these students enter the course expecting to fail, giving up becomes a very appealing option. To a large extent, each of these students needed the instructor—the authoritative expert (and evaluator) to say, "Don't give up." Julie's perspective in this regard was, "I know in the back of my mind that life happens and things may change, and [students] have to drop for whatever reasons, but my attitude is that everybody who enrolls, everybody, will pass."

Julie spoke of students who have come to her in the middle of the semester to tell her that they are dropping the course, with explanations about work conflicts, family crises, or other pressures in their personal lives. In those situations, Julie reported, she rarely concedes to students that dropping the course would be a good idea. She offered the example of one such student, whom she had advised not to drop the course midsemester. Later, the student had thanked Julie, saying, "I'm so glad you didn't let me drop." Julie concluded, "She just needed somebody to tell her that she could do it. Because if I were to say, 'Yeah, I guess you might want to drop,' then she would have felt, I think . . . [She left the thought unfinished.] I think it's important to hear someone say, 'That's really bad and I feel sorry for you, and that's terrible. But you can still do this. You can.' And she did."

Julie described all these efforts as her way of not letting students give up. Especially at Eastside campus, she explained, where students tend to be low-income and African American or Latino, generally first-generation college attenders, the stereotype is that most of them will not complete the course. But, she said, she rejects this position, because she thinks to herself, "Oh yeah? Well watch! I'm going to make sure that they succeed." And in the end, Julie's (and Beth's) more active approach to interacting with students led to higher completion rates in the Comp 1A courses.

According to the students in the two classes, the most significant outcome was pride at completing a difficult course and a new-found confidence about their ability to succeed. In Jenn's case, for example, she definitely learned "a hell of a lot" from the course. "Oh yeah, I definitely learned how to do a lot of things I didn't know how to do before. Like quotations and the works-cited list, and stuff like that. That's probably the only English class I've ever enjoyed in my whole entire life. And I've learned a hell of a lot more than I have in my whole years of school."

Like many other students across the six classes, when Jenn provided examples of what she had learned, she highlighted concrete facts and rules, such as the MLA citation rules, and proper use of punctuation.[8] But the most important part of the course for Jenn, the part she mentioned first, and with most passion, had occurred at the start of the course, when she had teetered on the verge of dropping the class. "Once I got my first paper accepted for English, I was so excited. It made me want to go and write some more. Yeah, it made me want to go and write some more, and like, after my first—no, second—paper my mom just told me, 'I don't think anybody's given you the chance to write. I don't think anybody's given you what you needed, to learn.'"

Through Beth's encouragement, and by working through each assignment, Jenn gained confidence that given future opportunities to learn, she will be able to succeed. For Jenn, success in

Comp 1A both depended on and consisted of gaining confidence and believing that she had the ability to succeed in college.

When I asked Charmaine what aspect of the course had been most important to her learning experience, she replied, "Julie's feedback is really important, because a lot of times when I'm writing, I'm thinking, 'Oh man, this is not going to be good.' And then she reads it and she gives it back to me, and she's like, 'Hey, this is great. You did it!' and it's just her feedback, and the one-on-one that I've had with her, that has also made the class."

For Kyra, who had "this total fear factor" about English, doing well in Beth's class provided evidence of writing competence. According to Kyra, "So that kind of in itself indicates that I'm not as bad as I thought I was. And my fear is maybe just in my head, rather than actual fact."

Even the students who had, at the start of the semester, experienced the most fear and loathing of English courses reached similar conclusions by the end of the course.

> I actually like writing. I actually like it! It's not as bad as it was in high school. It's not bad at all. It's actually nice. (Sarah)

> I hated writing, but now I feel that I know that I can. I feel better now. I'm not afraid like I was before. (Linda)

The reality of mass higher education is that not every student will reach the college classroom with the same knowledge, preparation, and expectations. Whereas selective programs and colleges can avoid addressing the issue, those with more-accessible entry points necessarily face the challenge.

The specific pedagogical strategies that Beth and Julie employed succeeded because they formed a coherent approach: expecting students to accomplish work that they found challenging; inviting them to participate actively as "college" students in the classroom; addressing students' anxiety with step-by-step, transparently clear directions; and offering constant encouragement.

Crucial to the success of their approach was having students achieve a certain level of comfort in the classroom environment. In other words, success did not result from the *use* of these specific strategies; success resulted from students' *perceptions* of the instructors' attitude and classroom environment. And for these students, recognizing and addressing the high degree of anxiety they felt was the crucial element in instructors' approach to shaping their students' perceptions. As I explored in Chapter 2, the intensity of the fear that students experienced proved overwhelming for many of them; as a result, the students needed a *lot* of positive comments in order to recognize them as encouragement or validation. Effective instruction clearly depends in part on teachers' understanding what constitutes "failure" for students, how small mistakes or confusion can confirm students' feelings of inadequacy, and how difficult it can be for many students to recover from academic mistakes.[9]

A significant aspect of Beth and Julie's success stemmed from students' trust in these instructors' professorial authority, in conjunction with the teachers' ability to address the "fear factor." Both women embodied the traditional professor's role as expert, authority, transmitter of information, while incorporating strategies that validated students' sense of belonging and while engaging in a more caring and personal relationship with students. In these ways, Beth and Julie created a learning environment that students perceived as encouraging. In contrast, other highly competent professors may have unknowingly contributed to students' tendency to avoid seeking help and to disappear quietly from the class. I do not mean to suggest that other instructors did not care about their students or did not demonstrate the same commitment to students' progress or success. All six LSCC professors in this classroom study, for instance, demonstrated optimism about students' potential to succeed; however, their optimism did not necessarily penetrate students' consciousness.

PART 3

GATEKEEPING

WHAT WE THINK of today as the fundamental features of college were institutionalized a century ago. In the midst of the profound social and economic changes at the end of the nineteenth century, the newly established universities in Germany became the model in the reinvention of American higher education.[1] The basic structures and processes of previously existing American colleges—from administrative organization to faculty hiring and promotion policies—were transformed. The practice of hiring tutors gave way to the hiring of full-time professors—scientists and scholars in the emerging academic disciplines. Departments formed around these specialized fields of study, managed the course offerings and programs of study, and became autonomous organizational units. This organizational arrangement remains entrenched and exerts a huge influence on the typical undergraduate curriculum, which Gerald Graff accurately describes as "a vast disconnected clutter of subjects, disciplines, and courses." The result is that students are responsible for finding coherence in what frequently appears to be "an endless series of instructors' preferences that you psych out, if you can."[2]

Official recognition as a postsecondary organization became dependent on new forms of accreditation; meeting or not meeting those regulations, in turn, took on greater consequences.

New policies and norms emerged from various sources, ranging from professional associations to philanthropic organizations.[3] This process, thanks to which colleges around the country developed and adopted similar practices, structured the entire field of higher education and granted the highest status to this newly invented form—the research-driven university or college. Accordingly, emulating the most prestigious offered a means of acquiring legitimacy or greater status and, in turn, of attracting support from private donors, and increasing student enrollment.[4]

These developments affected the undergraduate population in several crucial ways. First, the purpose of college was reformulated, made more relevant to the industrializing economy. The classical curriculum was phased out, in favor of a modernized course of study in the liberal arts and a burgeoning array of "practical" fields of study. By 1900, English studies had become the foundation of a liberal arts education, thus replacing Greek, Latin, and rhetoric. The new areas of study offered college graduates opportunities in the new economy and served as the stepping-stone to "professional" careers. Second, the changes introduced a greater measure of standardization for students, such as the definition of a college credit and a more consistent use of GPAs and class rankings. Third, colleges began to institute more stringent and standardized procedures for sorting students into appropriate programs of study. In other words, ideas about who should attend college and for what purpose were infused into university rules and routines. The most elite colleges led the way, by defining the highest-ranking students through admissions criteria and entry tests. Thus the "best" college students were those who made it through the most-selective procedures.

Selection and sorting procedures were represented as determining academic merit; however, the definition of academic ability was intertwined with other social considerations. Indeed, histories of this country's most selective colleges amply illustrate the role of social and cultural considerations in admissions decisions.[5] By 1920, for instance, two groups of aspiring college students—women and European immigrants (particularly Jews) —were considered less desirable, and elite colleges sought to limit enrollments from those groups or keep them out altogether. Moreover, even when such students were formally admitted, they were still excluded from full participation in college life.[6] To preserve their reputation, the elite colleges instituted recruitment strategies, entrance requirements, and admissions policies that barred entry to many students. New application components, such as interviews, photos, and mental tests, were used to select students with the right social background. According to the historian Marcia Synnott, Columbia University adopted Thorndike's psychological assessment in 1919 ("Tests for Mental Alertness") partly on the premise that "'objectionable' applicants would not have 'had the home experiences which enable them to pass these tests as successfully as the average native American boy.'" Synnott further reports that by the mid-1920s, "those Jews who passed the required academic and character tests found little or only a begrudging reception. . . . Jews were almost entirely absent. Jews, moreover, were often excluded from athletic teams of the major sports, debating societies, editorial boards, and musical clubs."[7]

The successful colleges were able to increase enrollment without risking their ability to attract the "best" students: male, white, Protestant, middle- and upper-class. Less selective colleges, however, faced a dilemma: if they wanted to increase student enrollment, they would have to admit some less desirable students. University leaders expressed concern that women would overrun the undergraduate programs; they also became concerned that high numbers of women would seek entrance to their graduate-level programs. Efforts were made to manage the influx of female students by confining them to fields already undergoing feminization: liberal arts, elementary education, and nutrition. The new research universities resisted admitting female graduate students; even when women did earn Ph.D.'s, their employment prospects were limited: they would follow a subordinate career path, whether inside or outside academe. Inside higher education, for instance, employment was available to women scientists as professors at women's colleges or at coed colleges in departments of home economics. Alternatively, women could find work as research assistants for male scientists. The professional societies for various sciences underscored distinctions between male and female members, through different levels of membership and men-only gatherings. For several decades, once women were no longer officially prohibited from attending these organizations' social events, de facto bans were accomplished by arranging "smokers" or encouraging members to smoke during particular discussions. Proper female deportment required that women avoid such events.[8]

Different colleges, as well as specific fields of study, earned a reputation based on the quality of the student population; schools with the greatest prestige devised sophisticated methods of screening and sorting students. Indeed, the most accessible entrance to higher education—the two-year college—originated as a means of screening baccalaureate aspirants. The earliest two-year colleges, established in Illinois and California, developed from the high school's "postgraduate" department and allowed students to take lower-division college courses. Through that process, the "best" students could be identified and allowed to pursue upper-division coursework, thereby preserving the academic standards of the four-year colleges. Students deemed less qualified could still complete a "terminal" associate's degree, which offered the possibility of entering the market for mid-skilled labor. The community college continues to play this role, by functioning, in the words of the sociologist Steven Brint, as the "midwife to humbler dreams."[9]

Today, strategies for selection and exclusion continue to operate throughout higher education. Formal processes such as admissions and entrance assessments, now based on more equitable standards of merit, do not discriminate against particular groups in the same obvious ways that they did in the past.[10] Informal practices play a gatekeeping role, however; these more subtle mechanisms favor certain students, not on the basis of academic merit, but on the basis of sociocultural advantages. One key example is the subject of the next chapter.

CHAPTER 7

ACADEMIC LITERACIES

"WHAT PERSON IN their right mind is going to sit there and basically analyze a movie, and get a point out of it?" For Jenn, this was a rhetorical question: according to her, no one in her right mind is going to think critically about a film, see meaning in it, and write about it. I suppose that Jenn would consider academics (or film critics) to be not "in their right mind," given that the exercise in criticism they routinely perform was the one that earned her complete scorn. Although she otherwise enjoyed Beth's English class and reported having learned a lot by taking it, she objected strongly to this one particular writing task: "When she had us write about the movie or the CD—oh, I found that so stupid. I found no relevance in doing it. It was just—I thought it was stupid."

Not only does Jenn's comment demonstrate the gap between her conception of appropriate writing tasks and the professor's expectations; it also illustrates a broader difficulty for students entering higher education. That difficulty is one of adjusting to the culture of academia.

Scholars from a range of disciplines have described the "culture" of academia in different ways but essentially agree that it involves particular habits of thinking, acting, speaking, and writing that are often incomprehensible and alienating to people outside academia. James Gee, a literacy theorist, has called this culture a Discourse (with a capital 'D') and noted that particular literacy practices are intertwined with beliefs and ways of thinking common to any Discourse. Students who are familiar with the norms of appropriate conduct and adept at adhering to them experience no problem. If a person has not assimilated or otherwise learned the rules, however, then the Discourse—as well as the specific literacy practices associated with it—functions as an obstacle to participation and success.[1] From years of teaching English to college students, Gerald Graff has identified the characteristics of academic Discourse that serve as the biggest stumbling blocks to students' productive engagement. One obstacle, he contends, is the dominance of what he calls argument literacy, which requires students to take positions and support them with persuasive reasoning. Another is the tendency of academics to discover or invent problems—thanks to maneuvers that appear to students exasperatingly pointless. Still another major impediment is the prevalence of abstruse and mangled language, which underscores students' perceptions that the topics under discussion are "remote and artificial."[2] Without explicit explanation (and translation), the academic conversation can easily remain unintelligible, irrelevant, and thoroughly unappealing. Unfortunately, explicitness is exceptional; the difficulty for the uninitiated of joining the academic conversation is exacerbated when professors assume that students understand what is expected. Consequently, students who are unfamiliar with the Discourse are often left to figure it out for themselves if they are to succeed.

For decades, scholars who do research on composition and literacy have documented the difficulties that college students have with argument literacy, or what is often referred to as critical literacy. In the 1980s, for example, Mike Rose examined the writing problems encountered by first-year college students at UCLA, finding that students could summarize and paraphrase texts, but could not engage in more analytical tasks. Rose clearly illustrated the ways in which prior schooling—"an inert transmission, the delivery and redelivery of segmented and self-contained dates and formulas" shaped their sense of academic work as requiring rote memorization rather than problem solving.[3] Once these students had entered college courses *unprepared* to do more complex work, faculty assumed that such students were simply *not able* to do it.

In the studies I have conducted, I have observed the same phenomenon among students. At LSCC, it caused confusion for students during the research paper assignment when the instructions directed students (whether implicitly or explicitly) to construct an argument—a task that they perceived as writing "opinions." This confusion emerged most clearly in Beth's class, because her instructions for the research paper explicitly asked students to write a "persuasive research paper." To many students in her class, this posed an impossible task. As Liz explained: "Oh, the class is just stupid. I mean, who wants to write a persuasive research paper? I still don't get that. I mean, I've talked to my boyfriend, who is an English major at [Flagship University], and he even said, 'Your teacher is stupid.' I mean, it's research; research is factual." Liz could envision providing facts about her research topic, but she was unable to understand how to construct an analysis or develop an argument using those facts.

Like Jenn's objection to the film analysis, Liz's complaint arose from disconnection from and unfamiliarity with the rules of academic discourse. The result, for Jenn, Liz, and others, was utter confusion about the purpose or logic of the writing assignment and their evaluation of the task as "stupid."

Similar writing difficulties emerged for students when they took tests. Mariella told me that she understood the material in her psychology course, but that on tests the teacher "came out with brand new things," such as scenarios that required students to apply the material they had learned to an unfamiliar situation. This Mariella found both confusing and unfair. Similarly,

Yolanda's description of her struggle with U.S. history exams suggests that Yolanda was missing an important analytic dimension during class lectures:

> I came in with the best intentions to do good in that class. He gives us a sheet of paper with all these names that he's going to talk about—George Washington, and la-da-da-da, Lincoln, and everybody—and he just jumbles it all up and when he says a name, you just better write. That's all you do throughout the whole class is just write. I mean, he's like, "And this is how this one ties in with this page, and this is how this ties in with this. And this is how this person comes in the whole play and this is how this whole Boston Tea Party came about." I mean, that's how he does. He gives what he calls a word list, and he just talks.
>
> And, you know, a lot of people have asked him, "Are you going to use the book?" He's like, "Well, if you study the book, and take the test, you'll be okay." Well, a lot of people took the test and if it wasn't for the thirteen colonies, the extra credit, everybody would have flunked. So he doesn't use the book whatsoever.

To Yolanda, her professor's lectures come across as a jumble of names and events. Despite writing everything down and studying the textbook, and above all wanting to do well in the course, Yolanda failed the first test. In her eyes, the problem was that the professor departed from the text ("He doesn't use the book whatsoever"), but I suspect that she faced a situation analogous to Mariella's, in which the exam required students to do more than memorize and regurgitate facts.

The end-of-semester tally for these three students was not all bad: Jenn passed her English course with flying colors, and Mariella squeaked by in psychology. Yolanda withdrew from the U.S. history course midsemester, however, to avoid failing it. Furthermore, by the end of the semester, Mariella was considering changing her degree plan from an associate's degree to a certificate program, so that she wouldn't have to take any more useless courses like psychology and English. Thus, for Mariella and Yolanda, the incomprehensible culture of academia functioned as a screening device, in essence hindering them from advancing toward their goals as originally intended.

Complicating the situation for the uninitiated is that the academic culture of higher education is not monolithic. Different fields of study have developed distinctive modes of inquiry and, as a consequence, different literacy norms. Although the fundamentals of traditional academic discourse may hold true across different disciplines, there are definite differences in what different fields consider acceptable writing practices. This means that a firm consensus does not always exist within the same college about what actually constitutes college-level writing competence. Generally, the lack of agreement among faculty members is apparent only to students, who, in the words of Gerald Graff, are forced to "psych out" what appears to be "an endless series of instructors' preferences."[4]

At several colleges I have visited, faculty members have voluntarily participated in efforts to improve writing instruction by developing specific criteria for assessing different levels of student writing performance. Even among instructors from the same English department, it can take some time and discussion to reach consensus on the criteria for different scores. In the case of a Writing across the Curriculum (WAC) initiative at one college, faculty members from different departments reportedly had wildly different expectations for the same first-year students. As one of the participants recounted, "They had us practice reading papers of what they thought was an entry [-level] student's work, and just trying to get the faculty on the right page in terms of how you assess these beginning students was a huge challenge."

A psychology professor at a different college illustrated the implications of this collegewide inconsistency with a short vignette. In her interview she recalled, "Last semester, there were four people in my class that I kept writing and saying, 'You really need to get a writing tutor.' And one of them came up at the end of the class, and she said, you know, 'I have had English composition. I got an 'A' in it.' But there must be ways to fake your way through. . . . Someone who's passing English 1A with an A, and they can't write an essay for your class? Somebody's lying." Using this specific example, the psychology professor made two points: one regarding the kinds of inadequate writing that she encounters from her students, and another about a potential problem with the English composition course ("There must be ways to fake your way through").

Of course, without more information about what the instructor meant by "can't write an essay," the source of this student's difficulty remains a puzzle; nevertheless, it is possible that the student, though capable of writing an adequate essay, did not understand the instructor's implicit expectations. It is also possible that the students in question were capable of writing good essays in the English composition class but were not yet adept at writing an essay on a psychology topic in accordance with the conventions in the field of psychology. Certainly, I have witnessed students who had been exposed in composition class to the style manual of the Modern Language Association (MLA) struggle when asked to work with the citation rules of the American Psychology Association (APA). The MLA rules are explicitly documented, whereas other conventions of essay writing are implicit, less straightforward, and learned primarily by exposure to the discipline.

A crucial point here is that many college faculty members, who have assimilated the discourse in their particular discipline over years of graduate study, take the rules for granted and can easily assume that entering students do so as well. This attitude presupposes that college-level writing is a straightforward skill to acquire, and that students should have attained such skills before entering discipline-specific courses in psychology, history, and sociology. Therefore, like the psychology instructor quoted earlier, such professors tend to diagnose the problem as a skill deficit instead of a result of conflicting disciplinary conventions or the inherent obstacles to acquiring academic literacies.

THE FALSE PROMISES OF COMPOSITION

The very premise for general writing courses such as composition is that students, once they complete their English composition requirements, will be properly schooled in the kind of writing required in the rest of their college courses. Research in cognition and learning over the past several decades, however, has demonstrated that this premise is highly flawed: skills and knowledge that an individual acquires in one context do not automatically transfer to new contexts. Indeed, applying skills in new contexts is extraordinarily complicated and is influenced by the learning environment in the original context as well as in the new context. At bottom it is unreasonable to imagine that a single writing course can adequately prepare students for all the writing tasks they may face in college.

Whether through familiarity with theories of composition or through experience, English teachers are likely to recognize the difficulty of transferring skills. Beth, for example, commented on the contradictions embedded in the composition requirement at her college. "I think Comp 1A is understood to be a preparation for further college work. It doesn't seem to me that it really promotes that purpose very well. It's hard for students to translate skills from an English class into history or philosophy."

At a college in Washington, a dean expressed this less traditional view, based on her experience with the health sciences. "Most college instructors think that if students test into English 1A, then they are probably ready for college-level classes . . . , but there has also been talk that 1A may not be sufficient. For example, in our area, we have a lot of medical programs. Sometimes I think there is a big mismatch there between what English 101 does and what the medical professions want their students to do as far as writing goes."

David Russell explains the large-scale problem that composition requirements engender: "The existence of separate and general writing courses encourages disciplines to mistakenly assume that they do not teach 'writing' but only 'content.' When some students cannot 'write' (by the discipline's standards), the fault must lie elsewhere: in the students who do not master the 'content' or in the secondary school English or college composition teachers who did not properly teach (autonomous) literacy."[5]

Paralleling the work in cognitive science, literacy studies have demonstrated unequivocally that the premise of generic or universal writing instruction is fundamentally flawed. As the researcher Tom Fox puts it, a general writing course, such as Comp 1A, "makes claims to a privileged place in the general education curriculum based on promises that the course cannot keep."[6]

One reason for this discrepancy is that the kinds of writing skills required in different academic disciplines vary immensely. But even within any given field of study, the standards for "good" writing in one context do not necessarily apply to other writing tasks. Writing skills—like any other skill—do not constitute an autonomous or generic tool, ready for application in any writing situation.[7] Instead, writing skills are integrally linked to each activity system in which they are used. A person does not simply write; a person writes something for some purpose. Accordingly, learning how to write according to the conventions of a particular academic discipline is best accomplished while a person is immersed in discipline-specific activities.[8] Similarly, studies demonstrate that learning how to write for specific professional contexts is most effective when it occurs at the workplace.[9]

And yet a flawed understanding of writing competence is thoroughly institutionalized—it pervades the entire structure of higher education. English composition, a firmly established requirement across most of higher education, constitutes the course with the highest enrollment of the undergraduate curriculum. Composition courses offered by two-year colleges are usually coordinated with those offered at the four-year colleges and universities. Consequently, community colleges are obligated to offer the course in a form that matches the four-year college version and are unlikely to adopt any approach that is significantly different from that used at the four-year colleges they feed. Yet in the absence of any other explicit and formally mandated writing instruction, English professors and composition classes become the sole guarantors for collegewide literacy and writing competence. In a telling example of the strength of tradition, the standard organizational approach to writing instruction had been altered at only one of the fifteen colleges in the national field study. That one college had recently instituted a Writing across the Curriculum initiative, in an effort to infuse discipline-specific writing instruction into a good number of courses. Significantly, this was also the only college that had examined the levels of learning attained by its graduates. Specifically, the college had undergone a campuswide assessment of students' progress from matriculation to program completion, which revealed discouraging results for literacy scores. As the respondent explained, before instituting the WAC reform, "What we found was that we had students coming in as freshmen reading above the norm at public colleges around the country. But after being with us for two years, the reading scores slipped. I suspected all along that there wasn't enough emphasis on reading. We have a lot of people here who are very fond of scantrons and multiple-choice exams. In my own class, I get students who say, 'There's so much writing here and reading. I didn't do that in my other classes.'" Thus this college was unusual on two counts: its efforts to identify what students gained by completing courses, rather than simply trying to identify the level of skill of its incoming students, and its experiment with WAC after administrators saw the results of the student learning assessment.

Administrators and faculty at all of the other colleges voiced concern about students' literacy skills and had made efforts to improve the situation. The changes adopted, however, did not target classroom-level learning. Following conventional patterns, the most frequent evaluation strategy was an examination of the cutoff scores on the entrance assessments for reading and writing, in order to determine whether the cutoff point should be raised or lowered. The second-most-common approach involved creating exit exams for writing courses. Some of the colleges instituted exit exams for the basic writing classes (at the precollege level), and others instituted exit exams for the composition course. Less frequently, additional support services might be supplied, most often in the form of extracurricular assistance (tutors, writing center improvements, and so forth).

In the end, to preserve the traditional way of doing things in this case means leaving an organizational problem for teachers to work out in their individual classrooms. A professor of history was one of many instructors who spoke of that challenge. She noted, "I have given whole lectures on how to write an essay to my class. And I'm a history teacher. But I say, 'Okay, this is how you write a history research paper. Or this is how you write an essay for my class. And this is how you write an essay for an exam.' So instructors just take it upon themselves to start teaching English in their classes, even though they're not English teachers. Because for one reason or another [the students] are not prepared." For this instructor, the burden of "teaching English" was wearying. She continued, "But I'm increasingly getting to the point where I feel like if you can't write an essay, you shouldn't be in my class." This presents a tough dilemma. On the one hand, this professor recognizes that students require further writing instruction to succeed in her class. On the other hand, offering the instruction herself calls for added time and energy on a level that is difficult—if not impossible—to sustain. In the absence of an organizational resolution, the default response is often to exclude students who lack preparation.

In fact, qualitative studies of community college classrooms reveal that the problem is one that college professors have been forced to address without organizational support for the past four decades. The typical faculty response has also been consistent over that period: teachers persist in lamenting the conflict they experience between accommodating "unprepared" students and maintaining rigorous standards. Community college instructors interviewed in the early 1980s, for instance, mentioned receiving mixed messages from college administrators: instructors were expected to teach "college-level" courses, yet to retain students who were only nominally prepared for college work.[10]

Faculty members generally interpreted the message as pressure to dilute standards in order for the college to enroll more students and thus receive more funding. Not only did teachers speak of the tension between open access and standards; they also revealed the lack of organizational support for dealing with that dichotomy. The administration suggested that faculty should maintain high standards while at the same time retaining students, but teachers did not know how to do both.

The concern with maintaining standards has not been confined to community college faculty. The demographic shifts of the college-going population that began four decades ago diversified the student population—both academically and socially—for all of higher education. Whereas traditional students had tended to graduate in the top third of their high school classes, increased access enabled individuals who ranked lower in high school to enter higher education. That these students would appear "less prepared" than their traditional peers was inevitable.[11] That professors would struggle in their efforts to educate these new students was perhaps also inevitable. In his observations at City College during the early 1990s, Traub proclaimed the failure of the City University of New York's open-admissions policy: "The academic handicaps that students were bringing with them to school were very, very stubborn. That was why . . . it was a matter of 'despair' for serious, dedicated teachers . . . that they could not solve the problems of students who had had so little experience of academic life."[12]

HIGH SCHOOL PREPARATION

It is easy to attribute students' difficulties to inadequate preparation at the high school level. Certainly, faculty members at every

college I have studied have identified poor high school preparation as a huge problem. Providing an example of the disconnect between high school and college, one professor pointed
out, "Eighty percent of our students place below college level in
math—and are unhappy about it, especially because a number of
them are transferring from a high school where 'I've had all this
stuff.' But they don't know it. I don't fault the high schools, necessarily. It's hard to teach people when they're more interested in
other things." Whether or not the high school is to blame for
students' inadequate skills, the students are viewed as deficient
once they arrive at college without having attained the expected
level of knowledge.

The reports students gave of their high school experiences revealed several kinds of problems. Some students, like Liz—who
contended that her high school was "really shitty"—had attended schools judged "low-performing" according to the state's
ranking system. Describing the characteristics of such schools,
students related tales of constant substitute teachers and regular
teachers who didn't care—who were only there "for the pay-
check." For some students, recognition of their school's poor
reputation made them less inclined to work hard.

But even for students who did not think of their high school
experiences as uniformly substandard, graduating did not presuppose a particular level of literacy competence. As noted earlier, Sebastian had been able to pass his English courses without
reading a single book. During senior year, Sarah was able to
avoid writing any papers for English. More than half the recent
high school graduates in Mr. Dobbs's composition course explained their understanding of a "research paper" as something
copied directly from an encyclopedia. Students offered example after example of inadequate opportunities to write in high
school. In addition, it is clear that many students simply do not
possess the kinds of critical literacy skills that college professors
expect.

From a different perspective, though, one could ask whether
students should be expected to produce college-level written

work before they have engaged in college coursework. This re-orientation of the discussion moves us away from thinking about what colleges believe high schools *should* be accomplishing and toward understanding what high schools *are* accomplishing.

A crucial element of the general context nowadays is rise of high-stakes standardized testing throughout the K–12 system over the past decade. The testing regime has shaped recent high school graduates' notions of appropriate writing in several ways.[13] For students in schools that have been labeled low-performing, the general trend in instruction has been driven by prepackaged curriculum kits and basic-skills exercises of dubious educational value. The kind of reading and writing incorporated into the tests has taken center stage in many schools, and preparing for the tests has displaced other aspects of the curriculum.

When interviewed for the national field study, faculty members at colleges in many different states lamented the effects of standardized testing on students' writing. English teachers in particular complained that the high school testing seemed to foster formulaic writing, in which students are more concerned with right or wrong answers than with developing an understanding of the text.[14] An instructor in Texas explained, "In high school—it's all about passing the high school exit exam, or whatever it is they're doing these days. And teachers come in and teach formulas for how to pass the test. There's a sense of condescension in saying, 'Okay, a real writer wouldn't do it like that, but if you follow this fake little framework, [use] this little crutch, then you'll be able to pass the test.'"[15] Another English professor noted, "They get so dependent on that structure. The structure seems to do everything it can to shut down thinking." Across the country, at a California college, an instructor reiterated the same observation about the crippling effect on students' thinking. "What's happening now in the K–12 system is that we have begun teaching to the state tests. And it totally destroys the whole critical thinking process. I know when I taught at Lincoln High

School, people would often tell me, 'Oh, it must be so wonderful to teach there because the students test so high and it's such an excellent school system.' Test scores were high because the students were prepared for a test. But as far as overall class performance, students would sit there for an hour while I talked. And if I asked questions, they would all just sort of stare at me. They had no idea how to actually think things out." In these ways, current policies governing the K–12 system may be increasing the gap between high school– and college-level academic expectations.

Instructors were not the only critics of the standardized testing regime. Jenn's critique of high school centered on teachers' use of time during class, which seemed to her to be overly focused on the testing standards: "Most of the teachers are so into the standardized tests and now they have all these benchmarks. We have to go about [meeting] benchmarks. We have to cover those for the benchmark, and it shouldn't be about that."

GATEKEEPING

Regardless of the policy climate in the K–12 system, the conventional solution in higher education to students without the desired academic competence involves gatekeeping. The most obvious gate is the external one: the admissions process. But no matter their level of selectivity in admitting students, all colleges possess gatekeeping mechanisms. Formal gatekeeping might take the form of entrance tests in math and English that prevent students from taking college-level courses until they complete some remedial work. Less-formal filtering occurs in introductory survey courses, which prevent a certain percentage of students from advancing to upper-division courses in the given field of study. General chemistry, college algebra, U.S. history, introduction to psychology: these lower-division courses frequently fulfill colleges' general distribution requirements, enroll large numbers of first-year students, and occasion the highest percentages of Fs and withdrawals. The amount of this kind of internal filtering is related to the accessibility of the college and is most pronounced at two-year colleges.

An English professor expressed one common stance toward such filtering: "The filtering process says to some of the students, 'You don't have the skills to do sophomore English courses, so go get the skills, or else do some other line of work.' And so we tend to get a better clientele in those upper levels. . . . [First-semester composition] really should be where you fish or cut bait." In this professor's view, the composition course affords students the chance to experience "college English." Students without the requisite skills might not attain them during the composition course, in which case they should "go get the skills" before moving on to more advanced English classes.

Describing himself as one of the "old farts" who has maintained rigorous standards over a long career in teaching, he said, "I haven't changed my standards. If a student is having trouble because of a job, early on, I'll say, 'Well maybe you could switch to somebody else's class.'" With this comment, Mr. Burke suggested that there are other faculty members (presumably the younger instructors) who *are* willing to compromise academic standards, and that the administration itself exerts pressure on faculty to lower expectations for students. In mentioning several speeches made by the president of his college, he interpreted the president's exhortations to boost enrollment and decrease attrition as indications that the administration wants the faculty to "lower the bar." Mr. Burke envisioned the kind of future driven by this attitude as a dystopia in which everyone who enrolled at Hillside would be coddled and passed along, so that enrollment numbers increased and thereby generated greater revenue for the "cash-starved administrators"—to the detriment of the academic programs. From Mr. Burke's perspective, if a community college is to offer a high-quality education, student attrition is a necessity. "Of course you get a group of kids who have no conception of what college is all about, who are interested in

partying, the opposite sex, and their job; and who[m] we lose—
I mean, we lose over half of the students; the administration
wants us to keep them. They want us to keep everybody—they
want us to give degrees to everybody, and screw that—I'm
sorry."

One of the most pervasive strands in Mr. Burke's implicit
comparisons was his perception of "college" standards: standards constantly at risk of being undermined by those who arrive at college unprepared to meet them. Faculty members representing every discipline expressed similar sentiments. At another
college, a math professor put it this way: "Some of us are—I
hesitate to say—more 'rigorous' than others. Some of us are
more demanding in our problems. I give really hard problems in
my classes. As far as I'm concerned, this is college. It's time you
learned to think on your own. And there are students who will
not take classes from me because I have a reputation as one of
the harder instructors on campus. On the other hand, we do
have a couple that they will take classes from because they're
more willing to slow down for the students, which I'm not."

Since the late 1800s, when Harvard instituted its entry-level
writing assessment and established its first-year writing course,
the traditional approach to ensuring students' writing competence has focused on regulating students' entrances and exits.
The easiest strategy is to exclude students before they enter certain courses, without restructuring the learning environment inside those courses. Over the past decade, as colleges have examined the results of their writing requirements and remediation
policies, the most common strategies for improvement have involved (a) changing the entry-level assessment tools, (b) adjusting the cutoff scores for placement in remedial courses, and (c)
developing exit tests for writing courses.

Monitoring admissions to the course and administering exit
tests are exercises in maintaining standards. These strategies cer-
tify that students who complete the course have gained the writ-

ing skills necessary for continued college coursework. When the same students do not complete future courses successfully, the English department can justify its instructional program with objective evidence that the students have met the required level of writing competence. College personnel can therefore account for students' failure by attributing it to students' own deficiencies (such as lack of effort, lack of motivation).

These strategies, however, fail to address the effectiveness of the classroom instruction, by neglecting, for example, to assess the extent to which the curriculum and pedagogy address students' "underpreparation," the growth in students' learning from the start of the course to the exit test, classroom-level dynamics that facilitate student success, or the specific reasons for students' withdrawals and failures. In itself, the failure to delve into these issues perpetuates the preexisting inconsistencies, which emerge as mismatched expectations on the part of students and instructors as students negotiate each transition—the transition into college, into college composition, and into the different fields of study.

CHAPTER 8

REIMAGINING COLLEGE FROM THE INSIDE OUT

SINCE THE 1960S, postsecondary study has become available to previously excluded groups of students. As we have seen, increased access has expanded the sheer numbers of students enrolling in college courses and broadened the range of students who attend. And yet, despite the tremendous changes in the demographics of students who have access to higher education, a huge gap remains between the number of students who aspire to college degrees and those who receive degrees. It is extremely significant that at the very schools where higher education is the most accessible, graduation rates are the most dismal.

The vast majority of high school students plan to attend college; indeed, it has become a stage in the transition to adulthood. At the same time, the growing importance of college as a gateway to occupational opportunity has increased the pressure to attend and the stakes of success or failure. Although many students are certain that college will differ dramatically from high school, they are not clear about specifically how it will differ. This is particularly true of those who represent the first generation in their family to attend college.

The studies I have conducted suggest that tacit, and in some cases very subtle, exclusionary dynamics are at work inside even the most accessible colleges. Students' conceptions—of college, of college professors, and of the role of a college student—govern academic performance at every turn. Producing adequate work requires that college students have the same understanding of "college" as the professors who assess their work. From this perspective, inadequate coursework—indeed, unacceptable college performance overall—results from something more complicated than a deficit of skills.

An example would be academic literacy (the subject of Chapter 7), which is acquired as much outside as inside the classroom. Inside particular classrooms, as discussed in Chapters 5 and 6, the complex interaction between instructors' intentions and students' expectations can limit the chances that students will accomplish their educational goals. First and foremost, the preconceptions students have about college and college instruction, as well as their underlying fear of failure, shape the college experience in fundamental ways, at times preventing learners from the kind of active engagement in their coursework that would be needed for them to succeed.

STUDENTS' EXPERIENCES OF COLLEGE

For students in these studies, college posed several related types of challenges. First, students believed that participation in higher education would be crucial to their future career success, yet anxiety about their abilities to succeed in college diminished students' willingness to slog through more schooling. Some students were prepared to quit, in order to avoid potential failure. As Jenn recounted (see Chapter 2), her immediate impulse after her first day of college classes was to drop all her courses. "I went to my first class, had like a four-and-a-half-hour break, and then went to my other three, went home, and I thought, 'I quit.'"

Eva described a similar panic attack during her first composition class, as we have seen: "That first day, when the professor said that it's going to be an essay after an essay, I was scared. I was like, 'Oh my God, I'm not going to be able to make it'" (Chapter 2).

Some students who started the semester with overwhelming fears were able to manage the anxiety and go on to complete their courses successfully. Doing so, however, required active intervention from someone at the college—someone who could reassure students about their academic competence and ability to succeed. For the students in these interviews, professors could play that role, especially when they were able to "come down to students' level" or if they were the kind of instructor who "really relates." Both Jenn and Eva benefited from having such instructors and by the end of the semester had earned As in the classes they viewed as most difficult.

In other cases, however, students faced a second obstacle: their feelings of inadequacy were easily exacerbated by respect for professors' mastery of the subject matter. For some students, recognition of professors' expertise increased their hesitance to seek the instructors' help. An extreme example of such avoidance was Colleen's admission about her approach to her philosophy instructor: "I sit in the back, behind whoever else I can find, so he doesn't even have to look at me. So I'm just kind of hiding in the back, thinking, 'Yes, I'm going to pass this class, somehow'" (Chapter 2). Countless times during my research, I spoke to students who were reluctant to seek professors' assistance, even after their professors explicitly invited them to do so. What was most confusing was that such hesitance did not reflect a disregard for the course or indifference to doing well. Instead, students' rationale for not approaching the professor was based on one form or another of fear-induced logic—like Elisa's protest that her professor would know how far behind she was on her paper if she were to seek help.

A third and related problem was that students' self-doubts severely limited their tolerance for confusing or unfamiliar activities and assignments. As a result, frustration with the level of difficulty of the coursework or confusion over the instructors' expectations for graded assignments could quickly drive students to the point of quitting. Most often, when students spoke of their confusion, they mentioned a specific assignment that was giving them trouble. Joy, for instance, who found that her English professor was insufficiently clear about what was expected, explained, "One thing I would like, though, would be, for the analysis paper—it's really tough for me because I've never done it before, and she sort of goes through it in class, but she doesn't really give examples on how to write it; like, she says, 'Discuss this, discuss that,' but she doesn't give an example on how to write it out—like, what's the format? How do you actually put those ideas into a format?—because I don't know. That's what I'm having a hard time with. I would hope that she would discuss that more."

Finally, as mentioned earlier, students' narrowly defined conceptions of "college" instruction and "useful" knowledge led them to understand the course content, assessment objectives, and classroom environment in ways that conflicted with instructors' goals. Many students, for instance, defined instruction that was not delivered in the form of a lecture as no instruction whatsoever. Students appreciated the professors' expert knowledge and thought of the instructors' primary task as one of explaining the information clearly. This meant that alternatives to the lecture format tended to be viewed as diversions or a waste of class time. Tied to this conception of teaching were the notions students held about knowledge and learning. For them, the value of the information (in the short term) was largely determined by the assessment procedures—the most important knowledge is whatever is essential to completing graded assignments. The kind of knowledge that students judged useful and relevant—Colleen's "informative information"—tended to be objective, concrete, and eminently practical. By contrast, exercises aimed at acquiring skills were often dismissed as uninformative and irrelevant.

STUDENT OUTCOMES

During the semester-long classroom studies I have conducted, I have observed a variety of student outcomes. First, a substantial number of students simply disappeared. For the most part, these were students who withdrew from the course well before the end of the semester. Some of the successful students I interviewed admitted that they had withdrawn from courses in previous semesters, and cited fear, feelings of being overwhelmed, and confusion about the assignments as their key reasons for dropping out. Perhaps some of the "dropouts" I observed have succeeded or will eventually succeed in passing the course—if something changes in their next classroom experience.

A second, much smaller category of students conscientiously attended class but did not submit the graded assignments. A few students failed to submit even one essay; more commonly, students submitted the first essay, which seemed "easy" to them, but then failed to submit any of the subsequent assignments. A third group comprised students who succeeded in passing the class. Of these students, some worked diligently to make the grade and learn the skills. Others decided—whether out of frustration with a "useless" course or out of lack of interest—simply to "get it over" with the minimum work necessary to receive a passing grade. At times, students seemed to decide merely to stick it out because they were not learning what they had hoped to or expected to learn. The experience made some students rethink their approach to the class as well as their long-term educational plans.

Jenn, Sebastian, and Melanie, the students whose experiences were highlighted in the chapters in Part 1, illustrate this range of outcomes. Despite her instinct to drop her comp class after the first day, Jenn persevered in the class. I suspect that had she taken the class with a different instructor, she might not have succeeded, but Beth, as we have seen, was one of the professors "who really relates." The combination of validation, challenging work, and explicit instruction that she experienced in Beth's class helped make the course "one of the best courses" Jenn had ever taken. She passed with flying colors.

Sebastian was a little more lackadaisical in his approach to his basic writing class. He felt that Mr. Burke was an excellent

teacher ("When he lectures, it's not like, 'Brother, this sucks'").
Even so, he admitted to being only "pretty motivated," not motivated "all the way." Consequently, he was not taking in all the
material; and though he was getting good grades, he wasn't getting As in the class.

In spite of her drive to succeed, Melanie did not pass her composition class. Although apparently "ready" and highly motivated to move through her college coursework without wasting
any time or money, she also expressed a great deal of anxiety
about the process. Like Jenn, Melanie was enrolled with a professor who related to the students, but Melanie was not able to
get past her fear of failing. The result was that she felt pressure
not to disappoint the instructors who seemed so committed to
her success. She told me: "I've realized that my teachers do know
who I am, and I am a very fine student. It's kind of reassuring,
and it's kind of rewarding, when they recognize who you are. . . .
But for me, it makes me feel really bad when I turn in a bad
grade, or if I don't turn in something good, because I really do
feel like I'm letting them down personally."

Melanie started falling behind during the weeks when the
class was working on the research paper assignment. She failed
to turn in the preliminary parts: a sample of notes and a bibliog-
raphy. She did submit a complete paper on time, presumably so
as not to disappoint her professor. Her professor, however, discovered that Melanie had downloaded it from the Internet, and
informed her that because she had plagiarized the paper, she
would not be able to pass the course.

THE CHALLENGES FOR COLLEGE PROFESSORS

In so many cases, ingrained conceptions about knowledge and
learning led students to understand and respond to course curricula in ways that were not easy for instructors to interpret accurately. At times, students' frustration with the inefficiency of the
instruction, the waste of time and money, and the irrelevance of

course content arose from lack of interest in the subject matter; at other times it signaled deep dissatisfaction with the opportunities for real learning—while reflecting very narrowly defined ideas about what constituted it. In the case of Mariella, her "bad attitude" about Comp 1A, as she herself described it, she attributed to her frustration with the course content and instruction. By the end of the semester, she had decided: "As long as I pass the class, I don't care. [pause] I shouldn't be having that attitude, but . . . " (Chapter 4). Once Mariella decided that she didn't "care anymore," she refused to participate in class discussions and expended minimal effort on the coursework (even graded assignments).

Teachers' lack of understanding of students' assumptions and motivations exponentially magnified the difficulty of teaching. When instructors recognized the reasons for students' lackluster performance—whether in class or on assignments—they were much more likely to be able to shape students' beliefs and behavior. Indeed, by virtue of their professorial authority, instructors exerted tremendous influence over students' sense of competence and willingness to seek assistance with coursework. Virtually across the board, an instructor's efforts to assuage students' fears functioned as an active invitation to take part in the class and marked the first step toward fostering the perception on the part of students that the coursework they were being asked to accomplish was challenging but "doable." In this way, the most promising pedagogical approach accomplished three crucial goals: it (a) demonstrated the instructor's competence in the field of study; (b) clarified both the instructor's expectations for student performance and the procedures for accomplishing the work; and (c) persuaded students that they were more than capable of succeeding. Achieving these results required that instructors be very clear and consistent in their messages to students and actively respond to their students' conceptions of the course goals, instructional activities, and learning strategies.

My research highlights the need for college educators to consider students' goals and expectations thoughtfully and systematically as they structure the learning environment in their classrooms. Uncovering and understanding students' preconceptions and expectations should take precedence in the process of rethinking learning objectives and the means of accomplishing them. Let me be clear: understanding students' expectations and preconceptions is not the same as adopting pedagogical strategies that confirm students' existing beliefs; but without a clear sense of what students expect when they enter college classrooms, teachers may find that their ability to challenge preconceived notions sufficiently to help students succeed may depend more on luck than on design.

INSTITUTIONAL OBSTACLES

Several features of American higher education discourage the kind of classroom-level investigation required to understand students' behavior and intentions. Those features serve to divert educators' attention toward less fundamental dimensions of teaching and learning. In the end these characteristics can be traced to a single source: the persistence of the professorial model.

The professorial paradigm remains embedded in a great many organizational practices, including two of the most powerful: faculty hiring and evaluation. Mechanisms that enable the college to influence faculty work, these processes of selection and socialization privilege the work of "professing" rather than teaching. The minimum criterion for employment as a faculty member, for instance, is a graduate-level credential in a relevant discipline, which serves as evidence that the teacher has a grasp of the disciplinary content. An instructor who has engaged in graduate-level study in an academic discipline has most likely been socialized in a research-oriented environment that values subject matter expertise and discounts the importance of pedagogy. Most often, too, those who become college professors enjoyed and excelled at graduate school, and they are motivated by intrinsic interest in their fields of study. Instructors' own academic orientation and experience inevitably shape their expectations of appropriate student behavior and "college" standards. As a result, it is very easy for new college instructors to enter their classrooms with expectations of students that do not match reality. Thus, although students can certainly be described as unprepared for college, the professors are not necessarily prepared for their students.

Within the English department at Lake Shore Community College, for example, at the time of the study over 60 percent of the full-time faculty held Ph.D.'s, primarily in the field of English literature (rather than composition or English education). Moreover, several long-standing members of the department spoke to me about the increasing necessity for full-time job candidates to hold an earned doctorate. In effect, this trend meant that full-time positions that became available in the 1990s were less likely to be filled by adjunct instructors in the department, who had teaching experience but tended not to have earned Ph.D.'s.[1]

Throughout the English department at LSCC—indeed, across all the academic departments at the college—the evaluation system also emphasized the notion of college instruction as professing. The end-of-semester course evaluations, for instance, asked students to rate their instructors on the clarity of their presentations and the kind of information conveyed.

Such items stress the role of the instructor as the one who presents and explains information and who focuses attention on pertinent information.[2] Embedded in all these organizational practices is a notion of professorial authority as founded on disciplinary knowledge and as corresponding to the model of "teaching as telling."

As for the teaching format, even the architecture of LSCC's classrooms set the stage for instruction by formal lecture. Although LSCC lacked the large auditoriums used for introductory courses at the nearby research university, the classroom spaces

Please indicate how frequently each of the following is true for this course:

The instructor's oral presentations and discussions are well organized.

never   rarely   sometimes   often   generally

The instructor explains the concepts and other related information clearly.

never   rarely   sometimes   often   generally

The instructor keeps the oral presentations and discussions focused on information relevant to the subject of the course.

never   rarely   sometimes   often   generally

8.1. Excerpt from end-of-course evaluation

were configured similarly to those, with rows of desks facing the instructor's spot—designated as such by the blackboard and large teacher's desk. Although the desks in most of the class-rooms were easy to rearrange, the default placement anticipated lecture-based instruction. Furthermore, only rarely did instruc-tors request students to reorient their desks to capitalize on the intimate scale of each room.

Students' classroom interactions and interview comments il-lustrated a whole range of ways in which their expectations and perceptions had been shaped by this persistent paradigm of pro-fessorial authority. Students' expectation that professors should dispense knowledge to the class, largely through lectures, was essentially confirmed by the organizational policies and struc-tures of the college. Once inside individual classrooms, students continued to understand the teachers' explanatory remarks as the most crucial component of instruction. Consequently, the al-ternative pedagogical approaches favored by a few instructors collided with both students' expectations and embedded institu-tional norms.

The assumptions underlying the professorial paradigm in fact reflect the three key elements students expected in the dynamics of teaching: the subject matter expertise of the professor, the clarity of curricular explanations, and the ability of the students to master the curriculum. This implies that teaching can be improved in three ways. First, the professor can improve or update his or her content knowledge. Second, the professor can reformulate the explanations of the curriculum, making them clearer and more engaging. Third, the student population can be upgraded through exclusion of the unprepared or less capable. In effect, college classrooms exist in an environment that underestimates the work of teaching—witness the assumption that proper curriculum content plus adequately "prepared" students equals a college education.

One consequence is a tendency to associate the value of the undergraduate program at a college with the status of its student population, rather than with the quality of teaching and learning that takes place inside the classrooms. The ability to exclude students thus brings greater prestige to a college. Not only does this circumstance doom the least selective colleges to the lowest perceived level of quality, but it has institutionalized the attitude that only an exclusive clientele can meet high standards. Using the status of the student population as an indicator of educational quality makes a certain amount of sense, for both the processes and outcomes of classroom instruction are difficult to articulate, isolate, or evaluate. But the effect has been to judge schools not by how much students learn in the classroom, but by how little (or how much) they need to learn before they enter college classes.

A second consequence of this conception of education is an unrelenting focus on the curriculum to be offered. Consistently, controversies over curriculum draw attention away from the processes of college teaching and learning, by focusing on *what* students should learn rather than *how* they will learn it. In fact, curricular debates tend to reflect conflicting conceptions about the broader purposes of a college education, rather than specific theories about learning and teaching. Scholars such as Larry Cuban and Derek Bok suggest that without more clarity and consensus about purpose, the most we can expect is incremental changes in the intended curriculum, without any real change in the learning that takes place.[3] Cuban specifically contends that tweaking the curriculum has allowed colleges both to attend to college instruction in a symbolic way and to negotiate compromises among interested stakeholders, all without addressing what really happens inside college classrooms.

Research has shown that the best college teachers understand how students learn, and are able to guide them from novice understandings of the subject matter to more developed understandings. Research in cognitive science has further made it clear that experts in any field organize and draw upon their subject matter knowledge entirely differently than do novices approaching the same material. Thus, simply having the expert's knowledge is not enough to be able to teach others. The education psychologist Lee Shulman has explored this phenomenon and has identified important distinctions between content knowledge and what he has termed *pedagogical* content knowledge.[4]

Whatever the conceptions of teaching and learning with which professors begin their teaching careers, it must soon become clear that subject matter expertise is not enough to make a person a good teacher. Learning how to teach depends on a process that Pat Hutchings and Lee Shulman (1999) describe as "a seat-of-the-pants operation, with each of us out there making it up as we go."[5] The best teachers have cobbled together—generally through trial and error—insights that match up with the research on how people learn. Of course, as Norton Grubb points out, this approach to learning to teach is not "particularly efficient, effective, or uniform."[6]

Furthermore, traditional postsecondary organizational structures hinder effective learning among the faculty. Colleges encourage faculty members to experiment and improve their teaching, but without reshaping the fundamental practices of faculty work. The pedagogical knowledge and expertise that professors develop individually remains hidden.[7] Successful pedagogical innovations flourish within hidden enclaves, but on the whole, college professors are left to interpret students' often inscrutable behavior, to invent and improvise solutions by themselves to fundamental and pervasive teaching challenges. The very organization of faculty work militates against substantial change and individual instructors remain responsible for addressing fundamental and widespread issues that cross classroom boundaries.

RETHINKING COLLEGE

Researchers and policymakers are currently focusing their attention on increasing individuals' "readiness" for college. These are admirable and much needed efforts. I worry, however, that "college readiness" efforts are based on unexamined assumptions about what today's college students "should" be prepared to accomplish before they even enter a postsecondary classroom. Perhaps more important, focusing on students' preparation takes attention away from students' opportunities to learn once they enter college. In the end, we can continue to view and treat the majority of college students as underprepared and unready, or we can revise our understanding of college, college teaching, and college learning. The discrepancies and contradictions of classroom practice described throughout this book constitute the fundamental (and unresolved) dilemma of educational access. Ultimately, improving students' educational opportunities depends upon first understanding their constructs of college more broadly—their imagined image of and responses to college, college professors, and college pedagogy.

Reinventing college to serve today's students better requires some redesign both inside and outside class. The fundamental goal of such redesign is to enhance the classroom learning environment for the students. This depends first and foremost on a vision of college teaching that is more sophisticated that the professorial model. A relational model, for example, highlights the relations students have to course content. In this model the instructor's primary task is to try to understand that relationship for all the students in the classroom, and to reposition students so that they can develop a new and different understanding of the course.

In the relational model of teaching, teaching is substantive, intellectual work, worthy of ongoing inquiry and experimentation. Application of this nontraditional conception of postsecondary teaching assumes that teaching is more complex than "professing" and that it is fraught with potentially irresolvable problems. Yet thinking of teaching as a practice that comprises inherent problems and ongoing tensions may expand the opportunities for productive inquiry. Such a view of teaching is at the heart of a growing body of research on teaching, known as the scholarship of teaching and learning (SoTL). This body of knowledge, as well as the conception of teaching practice underlying it, encourages a different approach to teaching improvement than does the professorial model. One component of good teaching, for instance, involves classroom-level study and action. More important, those engaged in teaching are also engaged in a learning project of their own. Taking students' learning seriously, as a matter necessitating careful investigation of students' preconceptions and expectations, requires adequate conditions for professors to learn about teaching the students who show up in their classrooms. Creating a learning environment for professors as *learners* calls for a different conception of faculty work; rather than working as individual, isolated faculty members, teachers should be given structured opportunities on an ongoing basis to learn through reading, writing, discussion, observation, and reflection with peers.

The task for individual departments and for colleges as a whole is to cultivate a learning environment for faculty members. Observers of the SoTL movement, such as Mary Huber and Pat Hutchings, offer a variety of practical ideas on how to do so; essentially, these researchers highlight the importance of creating robust opportunities to study teaching and learning and to engage in dialogue with colleagues.[8] Thus, supporting instructors' capacities at the classroom level requires serious organization-level commitment. First, enabling instructors to analyze and revise the learning environment necessitates significant and complementary resources: time and space to reflect, access to research literature, and departmental dialogue. Second, policies and practices need to promote consistency and coherence, in the service of investigating and challenging students' assumptions, questioning and reconsidering instructional approaches, and ultimately improving the educational opportunities for today's college students.

THE RESEARCH STUDIES

The research for this book comprises four studies. I conducted two of the studies by myself and was a member of the research team that conducted the other two studies. Together, these four afforded both depth and breadth. The classroom studies were critical to understanding the dilemmas that arise for both students and faculty members, because I was able to observe their behavior over time, in addition to soliciting their views and interpretations of the same events that I had witnessed. The large-scale multiresearcher studies allowed me to compare the perspectives of the faculty members and students in the classroom studies with those of professors and students across thirty-four colleges.

CLASSROOM STUDIES

I conducted two studies that focused on instructional dynamics at the classroom level. Both were semester-long studies that gathered in-depth, qualitative data. One focused on a basic writing course at Hillcrest Community College (HCC), a college in northern California (spring 2000); the other investigated six sections of English composition at Lake Shore Community College (LSCC), a multicampus college in the Southwest (fall 2002). In both cases, the objective was to identify the classroom-level conditions that facilitated students' successful completion of the course. To enable me to do so, the studies incorporated sustained classroom observation, several in-depth interviews with the instructor of each course, and interviews with a sampling of students from each course. From the seven classrooms, I interviewed a total of forty-one students, all of whom I also observed in class throughout the semester. In every case, the instructors had been identified by multiple measures, including community nominations and the receipt of teaching awards, as excellent writing teachers. To recruit students to participate in the study, I approached all students who were still enrolled and attending class during the last third of the semester. In most instances, the students went on to pass the course (with a grade of C or better), so my pool of participants was made up of successful students. The key difference between the two studies lay in the level of the English courses that the students were taking. The single-classroom study investigated a developmental writing class, one level below Comp 1A. Therefore, none of the students in Mr. Burke's developmental writing class had scored well enough on the college writing assessment to enter first-year composition without some remediation. In most cases, the students in the class had also been required to enroll in a separate basic reading class because of their scores on that entry test.   -

Nereida, Nola, Natalie, Nikki, Susan, Sam, Sebastian

A.1. Students in Mr. Burke's class

In contrast, the students in the study at LSCC had all been deemed proficient in the writing skills required to enter Comp 1A.

NATIONAL FIELD STUDY

This study was a large-scale investigation of fifteen colleges in six states. Conducted by the Community College Research Center at Teachers College, the project explored current concerns in higher education, such as state-led accountability, developmental

Alan	Beth	Julie	Lori	Michelle	Mr. Dobbs
Clay	Alicia	Charmaine	Joy	Ashley	Eliana
Mara	Jenn	Colleen	Luis	Carlos	Claudia
	Kyra	Diego	Maureen	Dennis	Hugh
	Liz	Eva	Miguel	Kevin	Mariella
	Ryan	Isabel	Ruth	Melanie	Paul
	Sarah	Linda	Suzanne	James	Talisha
	Serena				Yolanda

A.2. Study participants at Lake Shore Community College, by instructor

education, new postsecondary competitors, and Web-based education. The sample included rural, suburban, and urban colleges from six states with well-developed systems of two-year colleges: California, Florida, Illinois, New York, Texas, and Washington. Data were gathered over two years (2000–2002), and across the fifteen colleges. The interview respondents included 284 administrators, 278 faculty members, and 68 students. In order to construct a case study of each college, teams of three to five researchers conducted site visits over a period of several days. During that time, team members conducted one-on-one interviews and small focus group discussions with senior administrators, including the president, vice presidents, and deans; department chairs and program directors (for instance, the online education director and developmental education program director); faculty members from a range of disciplines, whether academic or professional and technical; and a few students who were enrolled in basic skills classes or in online courses. Because our research interests spanned multiple topics, in our fieldwork we gathered information from generally distinct parts of the colleges, including the corporate training arm, noncredit programs, and the gamut of for-credit programs. In addition to making the site visit, we gathered data from the institutional research office of each college and any relevant documents from the departments we surveyed. I personally visited one-third of the colleges in the study and was responsible for organizing and analyzing the data relevant to the online education topic.[1]

STUDY OF ADVANCED TECHNOLOGICAL EDUCATION CENTERS

This was a study of collaborative efforts among community colleges and neighboring four-year colleges aimed at developing innovative educational programs for training science and engineering technicians. The Advanced Technological Education (ATE) program is funded by the National Science Foundation (NSF), so all of the community colleges we visited were members of regional ATE centers that were operating through grant funding from NSF. The centers focused on one of three kinds of technological education—information technology, engineering technology, or manufacturing technology—and were engaged in efforts to create programs that (a) met some regional needs for a technical workforce and (b) would coordinate with local four-year college programs. Our study of the centers focused on organizational issues, including the strategies that the centers used to develop links between the community colleges and local industries, between the community colleges and participating four-year colleges, and between the community colleges and local high schools. Of particular concern to the centers was the potential for sustaining their efforts beyond the duration of NSF funding; therefore, a key dimension of the research was investigation of the centers' plans for institutionalizing innovative practices. The part of the study that I participated in included site visits to nineteen community colleges in five states, where interviews were conducted with students enrolled in the technology programs, participating instructors, and the program directors and other affiliated administrators at each community college. These data were collected from 2003 to 2005 by a team of five researchers (including me) from the Community College Research Center (CCRC). The final report detailing the findings of the entire CCRC study is posted on CCRC's website at http://ccrc.tc.columbia.edu/Publication.asp?UID=575.

NOTES

1. TODAY'S COLLEGE STUDENTS

1. This description was mentioned in two episodes of the Bravo Network's *Tabatha's Salon Takeover* (2008).

2. For this estimate, the most selective colleges are defined as the ones that admit no more than a third of the pool of applicants.

3. David F. Schaffer, "The States and Their Community Colleges" (New York: Nelson A. Rockefeller Institute of Government, State University of New York, 2008).

4. W. Norton Grubb, "Learning and Earning in the Middle, Part I: National Studies of Pre-Baccalaureate Education," *Economics of Education Review* 21 (2002): 299–321.

5. Bridget Terry Long and Michal Kurlaender, "Do Community Colleges Provide a Viable Pathway to a Baccalaureate Degree?" National Bureau of Economic Research, Working Paper 14367, accessed Feb. 9, 2009, at http://papers.nber.org/papers/w14367.

6. Kevin J. Dougherty, *The Contradictory College: The Conflicting Origins, Impacts, and Futures of the Community College* (Albany: State University of New York Press, 1994).

7. Stephen Provasnik and Michael Planty, "Community Colleges: Special Supplement to the *2008 Condition of Education*" (National Center for Education Statistics, 2008), at http://nces.ed.gov/programs/coe/2008/analysis/sa07.asp.

8. Furthermore, community colleges continue to expand their reach to various forms of academic and professional education. See, for example, Vanessa S. Morest, "Double Vision: How the Attempt to Balance Multiple Missions is Shaping the Future of Community Colleges," in Thomas Bailey and Vanessa S. Morest, eds., *Defending the Community College Equity Agenda* (Baltimore: Johns Hopkins University Press,

2006); Barbara K. Townsend and Jan M. Ignash, "The Role of the Community College in Teacher Education," *New Directions for Community Colleges* 121 (2003). During the 1990s, states such as California and New York exerted pressure on their higher education systems to situate all remedial courses at the community college level. During the spring of 2004 the governor of California announced that one component of state budget cuts would require the community college system to accommodate a certain percentage of students who had already been accepted at campuses in the California State (Cal State) and University of California (UC) systems for their first and second years of undergraduate coursework. Thus, the community college continues to offer a cost-efficient means of responding to the demand for higher education.

9. For an analysis of community college expansion in different state contexts, see Dougherty, *The Contradictory College.*

10. U.S. Census Bureau, Population Division, Census 2000 PHC-T-41, "A Half-Century of Learning: Historical Statistics on Educational Attainment in the United States, 1940 to 2000," at www.census.gov/population/www/socdemo/education/phct41. html.

11. John Bethell, *Harvard Observed: An Illustrated History of the University in the Twentieth Century* (Cambridge: Harvard University Press, 1998), 26–27.

12. Sara Goldrick-Rab, "Following Their Every Move: An Investigation of Social-Class Differences in College Pathways," *Sociology of Education* 79 (2006): 61–79.

13. Stephanie P. Choy, "Nontraditional Undergraduates," *The Condition of Education, 2002,* National Center for Education Statistics, NCES 2002 025 (Washington, D.C.: U.S. Government Printing Office, 2003).

14. For twelfth graders' aspirations, see "The Condition of Education" (2006), at http://nces.ed.gov/programs/coe/2006/section3/indicator23.asp. For the baccalaureate attainment of adults, see the U.S. Census Bureau Statistical Abstract, at http://www.census.gov/compendia/statab/cats/education/educational_attainment.html.

15. Howard C. London, *The Culture of a Community College* (New York: Praeger, 1978).

16. Mike Rose, *Lives on the Boundary: The Struggles and Achievements of America's Underprepared* (New York: Free Press, 1989).

17. W. Norton Grubb and others, *Honored but Invisible: An Inside Look at Teaching in Community Colleges* (New York: Routledge, 1999), 220.

18. See, for example, Michael W. Kirst and Andrea Venezia, eds., *High School to College: Improving Opportunities for Success in Postsecondary Education* (San Francisco: Jossey-Bass, 2004).

19. See, for example, Glynda Hull and others, "Remediation as Social Construct: Perspectives from an Analysis of Classroom Discourse," *College Composition and Communication* 42 (1991): 299–329.

20. James A. Berlin, "Contemporary Composition: The Major Pedagogical Theories," *College English* 44 (1982): 765–777.

21. George Hillocks, *Ways of Thinking, Ways of Teaching* (New York: Teachers College Press, 1999).

22. London, *Culture of a Community College;* Grubb and others, *Honored but Invisible.*

23. Ken Bain, *What the Best College Teachers Do* (Cambridge: Harvard University Press, 2004).

24. Diana Laurillard, *Rethinking University Teaching: A Framework for the Effective Use of Educational Technology* (London: Routledge, 1993), 3.

25. This expectation resembles Lani Guinier and her co-researchers' assertions about women students at elite law schools: "Formerly all-male institutions cannot incorporate and take advantage of difference without changing from within. We argue that by reconsidering [their fairness and functionality,] these institutions can transform themselves to benefit women, others who have historically been outsiders, and most importantly, all consumers of their services." Lani Guinier, "Why Isn't *She* President?" in Lani Guinier, Michelle Fine, and Jane Balin, eds., *Becoming Gentlemen: Women, Law School, and Institutional Change* (Boston: Beacon, 1997), 1.

26. For details about each of the research studies, see the appendix. Taken together, the studies examined the perspectives of students, faculty members, and administrators from thirty community colleges across eight states. Two of the studies relied primarily on interviews and archival data; the other two incorporated interviews as well as classroom observations over an entire semester.

PART 1: STUDENTS

1. For an excellent analysis of the contradictory components of the community college, see Kevin J. Dougherty, *The Contradictory College: The Conflicting Origins, Impacts, and Futures of the Community College* (Albany: State University of New York Press, 1994).

2. THE STUDENT FEAR FACTOR

1. On the extent of a "college-going culture" within different high schools, see Patricia M. McDonough, *Choosing Colleges: How Social Class and Schools Structure Inequality* (Albany: State University of New York Press, 1997).

2. For another discussion of fear and failure, see David Cannon, "Learning to Fail: Learning to Recover," in Moira Peelo and Terry Wareham, eds., *Failing Students in Higher Education* (Philadelphia: Open University Press, 2002). Another large body of psychological research on student motivation takes students' orientation into account (by looking, for example, at "failure-threatened students"). See Martin Covington, "A Motivational Analysis of Academic Life in College," in Raymond P. Perry

and John C. Smart, eds., *Effective Teaching in Higher Education: Research and Practice* (New York: Agathon, 1997).

3. My thinking has been greatly influenced by Erving Goffman's article "Cooling the Mark Out: Some Aspects of Adaptation to Failure," *Psychiatry* 15 (November 1952): 451–463. In particular, Goffman's categorization of defenses against failure provided the basis for my own discussion of students' fear management strategies.

4. Across community colleges in different states, composition courses account for the largest enrollment numbers, yet these courses also generate a high noncompletion rate. At LSCC, the passing rate for Composition 1A hovers around 60 percent. In other words, despite having been assessed as academically "ready" for college-level English, 40 percent of the students enrolled in Comp 1A consistently fail to complete the course with a grade of C or better. This rate of failure, which is significantly higher than that for most other courses at the college, highlights the gatekeeping role the composition course plays within the college. The scope of student failure in Comp 1A represents, albeit on a smaller scale, the contradictions in the community college mission to provide broad access to higher education.

5. This phenomenon parallels the findings in Ann Penrose's study of first-generation college students' perceptions and performance. In comparing first-generation students at a four-year college to their more "traditional" peers, Penrose found a higher level of self-doubt in first-generation students' self-assessments of their reading and writing skills. In the end, she concludes: "First-generation students' self-assessments indicate that, on average, they have less confidence in their verbal abilities than students [do whose parents went to college], even though the performance data demonstrate that this concern is unwarranted" (457). Ann M. Penrose, "Academic Literacy Perceptions and Performance: Comparing First-Generation and Continuing-Generation College Students," *Research in the Teaching of English* 36 (2002): 437–461.

6. Michelle's course grading system included a series of open-note quizzes on material covered during her lectures. Two-thirds of the way through the semester, she calculated students' quiz grades and recommended to students who were earning lower than a C that they withdraw from the course. Carlos was asked to withdraw on this basis—he had submitted his writing assignments but had not passed the set of quizzes.

7. As Patricia Cross noted, one of the unintended lessons they had learned was "that failure [was] always reaching out to envelop them" (22); they may become "failure-threatened" as a result. Reactions to the fear of failure include: avoiding tasks whose outcome is uncertain: selecting easy tasks or impossibly hard ones, where failure is assured (23). "Rather than seeing effort and success as related, they see effort and failure as related" (27). K. Patricia Cross, *Beyond the Open Door: New Students to Higher Education* (San Francisco: Jossey-Bass, 1971).

3. STUDENT ASPIRATIONS

1. Interestingly, Miguel had not been aware that the military would pay for his college degree until several years after he completed his service and decided to continue his education.

2. Csikszentmihalyi and Schneider in their 2000 book report the results of their longitudinal investigation of career development plans among teens, in which the authors followed the progress of a thousand students from sixth through twelfth grade in thirteen school districts. Mihaly Csikszentmihalyi and Barbara Schneider, *Becoming Adult: How Teenagers Prepare for the World of Work* (New York: Basic Books, 2000), 163.

3. In contrast, Yolanda's "big beef" about her history course was that the instructor had required a textbook but never "cracked it open."

4. "HOW IS THAT HELPING US?"

1. Rebekah Nathan, *My Freshman Year: What a Professor Learned by Becoming a Student* (Ithaca, N.Y.: Cornell University Press, 2005), 138.

2. David F. Labaree, *How to Succeed at School without Really Learning: The Credentials Race in American Education* (New Haven, Conn.: Yale University Press, 1997).

3. Note the following description of community college classrooms where teachers do not "socialize students to participate in a certain way": Students "fail to do assignments; they operate in 'lecture mode,' failing to retain information for very long; they spend endless amounts of time quibbling about the requirements of classes; they fill up class time with irrelevant personal stories and unrelated questions. These ways of undermining learning . . . are often deeply bred into students by years of K–12 education." W. Norton Grubb and others, *Honored but Invisible: An Inside Look at Teaching in Community Colleges* (New York: Routledge, 1999), 94.

4. Howard S. Becker, Blanche Geer, and Everett C. Hughes, *Making the Grade: The Academic Side of College Life* (New Brunswick, N.J.: Transaction, 1995).

5. Ibid., 133. Other researchers, in documenting the consequences for higher-achieving students in more competitive academic environments, illustrate how easily students' strategies for "doing school" can turn into a competition for grades that is stripped of real learning or intellectual engagement. See especially Denise C. Pope, *Doing School: How We Are Creating a Generation of Stressed-Out, Materialistic, and Miseducated Students* (New Haven, Conn.: Yale University Press, 2003).

6. At the same time, these researchers make clear, grading systems present different situations for students in different tiers of higher education. Dividing students into three groups according to ability, Becker, Geer, and Hughes describe the following scenario for students in the lowest third, "for whom the challenge of course work and grades seems to be too much." These students "either fail and leave school or

work desperately and thereby manage to barely meet minimum requirements. . . . Their objections to the present system, if they were voiced, would revolve around the onerousness of the sanctions and the limitations it imposes on their other activities. Many of these students, however, accept the system so completely that they do not question it sufficiently to consider such heresies. They attribute their difficulties to their own failings." Becker, Geer, and Hughes, *Making the Grade,* 145.

7.   Howard S. Becker, Blanche Geer, Everett C. Hughes, and Anselm L. Strauss, *Boys in White: Student Culture in Medical School* (New Brunswick, N.J.: Transaction, 1968), 117, 120.

8.   Labaree, *How to Succeed at School without Really Learning.*

9.   The pass-fail test at LSCC was the end-of-semester, formally proctored writing test that verified that students had successfully met the minimum standards for passing the course. The exam thus functioned as a basic test of competency. Students unable to pass the test would not receive a passing grade for Comp 1A, so although the standards were minimal, the stakes were high.

10. Gerald Graff, *Clueless in Academe: How Schooling Obscures the Life of the Mind* (New Haven, Conn.: Yale University Press, 2003), 67.

PART 2: CLASSROOM DYNAMICS

1.   I have relied on the following references for this synopsis: Geraldine J. Clifford and James Guthrie, *Ed School: A Brief for Professional Education* (Chicago: University of Chicago Press, 1988); Julie Reuben, *The Making of the Modern University* (Chicago: University of Chicago Press, 1996); John Rury, *Education and Women's Work: Female Schooling and the Division of Labor in Urban America, 1870–1930* (Albany, N.Y.: State University of New York Press, 1991); and Myra H. Strober and David Tyack, "Why Do Women Teach and Men Manage? A Report on Research on Schools," *Signs: Journal of Women in Culture and Society* 5 (1980): 494–503. See also Ellen C. Lagemann, *An Elusive Science: The Troubling History of Education Research* (Chicago: University of Chicago Press, 2000); and Margaret W. Rossiter, *Women Scientists in America: Struggles and Strategies to 1940* (Baltimore: Johns Hopkins University Press, 1982).

5. COLLEGE TEACHING

1.   These two instructors—both of whom had Ph.D. degrees—differed in their preferred form of address. The instructor I refer to as Beth invited her students to address her by her first name. In contrast, the instructor I have called Lori Brown asked that students use the title "Dr." Dr. Brown viewed this form of address as a sign of respect for her educational accomplishments. She indicated to me during an interview that "Doctor" carries a social meaning that distinguishes it from "Professor," a form of address Dr. Brown eschewed as being too "formal." In the case of the third instructor who taught at the Far North campus, whom I refer to as Michelle, she invited

students to call her Michelle, but students tended to prefer the alternative she had offered, "Mrs. Davies."

2. Paul Ramsden, *Learning to Teach in Higher Education* (New York: Routledge, 1992).

3. Ibid. With regard to the teaching orientations of elementary school teachers, see Paul Ammon and Allen Black, "Developmental Psychology as a Guide for Teaching and Teacher Preparation," in Nadine Lambert and Barbara McCombs, eds., *How Students Learn: Reforming Schools through Learner-Centered Education* (Washington, D.C.: American Psychological Association, 1998). Examples from higher education are reviewed in Michael Prosser and Keith Trigwell, *Understanding Learning and Teaching: The Experience in Higher Education* (Philadelphia: Open University Press, 1999).

4. The traditional conception encourages those studying postsecondary classrooms to examine one of three distinct aspects: the professor, the curriculum, or the students. Within this paradigm, the study of college teaching tends to focus on the professor or the curriculum. Research on the role of the professor tends to focus on whether the professor maintains expertise in a specialized field of knowledge and is able to organize and explain the material in a way that engages students. Examination of the explicit, documented curriculum is of key significance in this paradigm. Indeed, a large proportion of the discussion of postsecondary teaching has focused on curriculum, often seen as distinct from educational goals and pedagogy. As a result, such discussions neglect the domain of classroom-level interactions.

5. George Hillocks, *Ways of Thinking, Ways of Teaching* (New York: Teachers College Press, 1999).

6. These numbers correspond to the broader pattern at LSCC and other community colleges: community colleges enroll more women than men; men are also more likely to drop classes than women are. This phenomenon may be a result of simple economics: the opportunity cost of schooling tends to be higher for male students, and the subbaccalaureate degree offers fewer rewards for men than for women. The discrepancy may also, however, reflect the more negative K–12 experience for particular male students. Several studies have examined the intersections of race, class, and gender and the resulting differences in the experiences of schooling between male and female students in the same classrooms. See, for example, Nancy Lopez, *Hopeful Girls, Troubled Boys: Race and Gender Disparity in Urban Education* (New York: Routledge, 2003). For a study focused on boys' experiences with attaining literacy, see Michael W. Smith and Jeffrey D. Wilhelm, *Reading Don't Fix No Chevys: Literacy in the Lives of Young Men* (Portsmouth, N.H.: Heinemann, 2002).

7. See, for example, Christine M. Cress and Jennifer L. Hart, "Are Women Faculty Just 'Worrywarts'? Accounting for Gender Differences in Self-Reported Stress," *Journal of Human Behavior in the Social Environment* 17 (2008): 175–193.

8. See, for example, Dale Bauer and Katherine Rhoades, "The Meanings and Metaphors of Student Resistance" in Veve Clark, Shirley N. Garner, Margaret Higonnet, and Ketu Katrak, eds., *Antifeminism in the Academy* (New York: Routledge, 1996). See also Frances A. Maher and Mary Kay Tetreault, *The Feminist Classroom* (New York: Basic Books, 1994).

9. For several telling examples, see the case studies in Mary T. Huber, *Balancing Acts: The Scholarship of Teaching and Learning in Academic Careers* (Washington, D.C.: American Association for Higher Education and Carnegie Foundation for the Advancement of Teaching, 2004).

10. Tom Fox, *The Social Uses of Writing: Politics and Pedagogy* (Norwood, N.J.: Ablex, 1990), 42.

11. Beth had structured the peer review component of the course very carefully. She created small groups on the basis of students' responses to a questionnaire about their perceived strengths and weaknesses in revising and editing, in an effort to balance the groups in such a way that each comprised a range of strengths. For the first small-group activity, students read each other's drafts for paper 1, in a low-key introduction to their peers' writing. Later, in preparation for the next group session, she distributed a list of criteria for providing feedback on rough drafts and talked through the process of sharing "respectful" and constructive comments on works-in-progress.

6. PROFESSORS WHO "COME DOWN TO OUR LEVEL"

1. For instance, Rhona Weinstein's research on K–12 classrooms underscores the role of teachers' optimism in helping less advantaged students achieve academic success. Rhona Weinstein, *Reaching Higher: The Power of Expectations in Schooling* (Cambridge: Harvard University Press, 2002). The importance of optimism is also a key finding in George Hillocks's 1999 study of community college English instructors. George Hillocks, *Ways of Thinking, Ways of Teaching* (New York: Teachers College Press, 1999).

2. I observed both short interactions and longer consultations between instructors and students. These took place in a variety of contexts, some during "workdays" dedicated to individual conferences, some in individual classrooms either before or after class sessions, others outside class time, at instructors' offices, and still others at the different campus writing centers.

3. Across the six classes observed at LSCC, the successful completion rate or "mastery rate," at 63 percent, was only slightly higher than the department average.

4. For a theoretical discussion of "relational authority," see Barbara Applebaum, "On Good Authority, or Is Feminist Authority an Oxymoron?" *Philosophy of Education Society Yearbook* (1999), accessed Feb. 12, 2009, at www.ed.uiuc.edu/eps/PES-Yearbook/1999/applebaum_body.asp; and Maureen Ford, "Shifting the Authority Project," *Philosophy of Education Society Yearbook* (1999), accessed April 8, 2009, at www.ed.uiuc.edu/eps/PES-Yearbook/1999/ford.asp.

5. Laura I. Rendon, Romero E. Jalomo, and Amoury Nora, "Theoretical Considerations in the Study of Minority Student Retention in Higher Education," in John M. Braxton, ed., *Reworking the Student Departure Puzzle* (Nashville, Tenn.: Vanderbilt University Press, 2002).

6. Susan E. Moreno and Chandra Muller, "Success and Diversity: The Transition through First-Year Calculus in the University," *American Journal of Education* 108, no. 1 (November 1999): 30–57, quotation on 33.

7. For a well-articulated critique of the "person-centered" perspective, see Rendon, Jalomo, and Nora, "Theoretical Considerations."

8. Interestingly, when students reported that they had become more skilled at the actual process of writing, they attributed that improvement simply to the opportunity to practice writing, and not to anything they had learned from taking the class.

9. David Cannon, "Learning to Fail: Learning to Recover," in Moira Peelo and Terry Wareham, eds., *Failing Students in Higher Education* (Philadelphia: Open University Press, 2002).

PART 3: GATEKEEPING

1. I have drawn on the following sources in writing this historical account: Geraldine J. Clifford and James Guthrie, *Ed School: A Brief for Professional Education* (Chicago: University of Chicago Press, 1988); Larry Cuban, *How Scholars Trumped Teachers: Change without Reform in University Curriculum, Teaching and Research, 1890–1990* (New York: Teachers College Press, 2000); Julie Reuben, *The Making of the Modern University* (Chicago: University of Chicago Press, 1996); Frederick Rudolph, *Curriculum: A History of the Undergraduate Course of Study since 1636* (San Francisco: Jossey-Bass, 1977); Lawrence R. Veysey, *The Emergence of the American University* (Chicago: University of Chicago Press, 1965).

2. Gerald Graff, *Clueless in Academe: How Schooling Obscures the Life of the Mind* (New Haven, Conn.: Yale University Press, 2003), 3, 67.

3. Established in 1905, the Carnegie Foundation for the Advancement of Teaching was a powerful force in the standardization and centralization of higher education. The foundation was charged, for example, with the task of administering a pension fund for college professors. By explicitly defining who qualified for the program—which developed into Teachers Insurance and Annuity Association (TIAA)—the Carnegie Foundation in effect assumed authority for determining the components of a legitimate college or university. For a compelling discussion of the ways in which elite educators used the foundation to institute a particular vision of higher education, see Ellen C. Lagemann, *Private Power for the Public Good: A History of the Carnegie Foundation for the Advancement of Teaching* (Middletown, Conn.: Wesleyan University Press, 1983).

4. For a theoretical discussion of this structuring process, see Paul J. DiMaggio and Walter W. Powell, "The Iron Cage Revisited: Institutional Isomorphism and Collec-

tive Rationality in Organizational Fields," in Powell and DiMaggio, eds., *The New Institutionalism in Organizational Analysis* (Chicago: University of Chicago Press, 1991).

5. This observation is from Marcia G. Synnott, "The Admission and Assimilation of Minority Students at Harvard, Yale, and Princeton, 1900–1970," in B. Edward McClellan and William J. Reese, eds., *The Social History of American Education* (Urbana: University of Illinois Press, 1988); for other accounts of exclusionary efforts, see Clifford and Guthrie, *Ed School;* Roger L. Geiger, "Markets and History: Selective Admissions and U.S. Higher Education since 1950," *History of Higher Education Annual* 20 (2000): 93–108; Jerome Karabel, *The Chosen: The Hidden History of Admission and Exclusion at Harvard, Yale, and Princeton* (Boston: Houghton Mifflin, 2005); and Ira Katznelson, *When Affirmative Action Was White: An Untold History of Racial Inequality in Twentieth-Century America* (New York: Norton, 2005).

6. Karabel, *The Chosen.*

7. Synnott, "Admission and Assimilation," 317, 321.

8. Margaret W. Rossiter, *Women Scientists in America: Struggles and Strategies to 1940* (Baltimore: Johns Hopkins University Press, 1982), 92.

9. Steven Brint, "Few Remaining Dreams: Community Colleges since 1985," *Annals of the American Academy of Political and Social Science* 586 (2003): 16–37, quotation on 32.

10. But as the sociologist Jerome Karabel has pointed out, students from stronger socioeconomic backgrounds have the advantage in the current selection processes, "for by conventional definitions, the privileged *are* the meritorious; of all students nationwide scoring over 1300 on the SAT, 66 percent come from the top socioeconomic quartile and only 3 percent from the bottom quartile." Karabel, *The Chosen,* 554.

7. ACADEMIC LITERACIES

1. James P. Gee, *Social Linguistics and Literacies: Ideology in Discourses* (London: Taylor and Francis, 1996).

2. Gerald Graff, *Clueless in Academe: How Schooling Obscures the Life of the Mind* (New Haven, Conn.: Yale University Press, 2003), 3, 23–25.

3. Mike Rose, *Lives on the Boundary: The Struggles and Achievements of America's Underprepared* (New York: Free Press, 1989), 190.

4. Graff, *Clueless in Academe,* 67.

5. David Russell, "Activity Theory and Its Implications for Writing Instruction," in Joseph Petraglia, ed., *Reconceiving Writing, Rethinking Writing Instruction* (Mahwah, N.J.: Lawrence Erlbaum, 1995), 67.

6. Tom Fox, *Defending Access: A Critique of Standards in Higher Education* (Portsmouth, N.H.: Boynton/Cook, 1999), 54.

7. For examples of scholarship on social cognition that addresses the issue of transfer of skill more broadly, see John S. Brown, Allan Collins, and Paul Duguid, "Situated Cognition and the Culture of Learning," *Educational Researcher* 18 (1989): 32–42; Jean Lave and Etienne Wenger, *Situated Learning: Legitimate Peripheral Participation* (Cambridge: Cambridge University Press, 1991); and Barbara Rogoff, *Apprenticeship in Thinking: Cognitive Development in Social Context* (New York: Oxford University Press, 1990). The very existence of such courses perpetuates the "general writing skills" myth, which David Russell defines as "the false notion that there can exist 'good writing' independent of an activity system that judges the success of a text by its results within that activity system, and that the teaching and learning of such writing can be divorced from any activity system beyond [general writing skills instruction]." Russell, "Activity Theory and Its Implications," 60.

8. See, for example, Petraglia, *Reconceiving Writing;* and Katherine L. Weese, Stuart Greene, and Stephen L. Fox, "Introduction: The Value of the University of Wisconsin-Madison's First-Year Writing Curriculum," in Katherine L. Weese, Stephen L. Fox, and Stuart Greene, eds., *Teaching Academic Literacy: The Uses of Teacher-Research in Developing a Writing Program* (Mahwah, N.J.: Lawrence Erlbaum, 1999).

9. Relevant examples include Patrick Dias, *Worlds Apart: Acting and Writing in Academic and Workplace Contexts* (Mahwah, N.J.: Lawrence Erlbaum, 1999); and Rachel Spilka, *Writing in the Workplace: New Research Perspectives* (Carbondale, Ill.: Southern Illinois University Press, 1993).

10. Earl Seidman, *In the Words of the Faculty: Perspectives on Improving Teaching and Educational Quality in Community Colleges* (San Francisco: Jossey-Bass, 1985).

11. Researchers contended that giving these less "prepared" students a second chance for educational success would require innovative pedagogical approaches, something different from their prior academic experiences.

12. James Traub, *City on a Hill: Testing the American Dream at City College* (Reading, Mass.: Addison-Wesley, 1994), 207.

13. George Hillocks, *The Testing Trap: How State Writing Assessments Control Learning* (New York: Teachers College Press, 2002); Diana Rhoten and others, "The Conditions and Characteristics of Assessment and Accountability: The Case of Four States," in Martin Carnoy, Richard Elmore, and Leslie Santee Siskin, eds., *The New Accountability: High Schools and High-Stakes Testing* (New York: RoutledgeFalmer, 2003).

14. In a telling interview example, an instructor at a Florida community college was asked: "Since the state started tests for success for high school, did that create students who were better in math from before a few years ago?" In reply, the instructor asserted, "I think they're teaching to the test. So the kids get through the test but then they don't really learn it well."

15. This attitude stood in contrast to his own objectives, which he described like this: "I don't like to condescend to students. . . . ultimately, they need to learn to do things on their own. I need to provide them the skills for them to become learners for themselves."

8. REIMAGINING COLLEGE FROM THE INSIDE OUT

1. Between 1997 and 2002, 60 percent of the newly hired full-time faculty had Ph.D.'s. This indicates not a trend toward hiring *more* Ph.D.'s, but a continuing trend toward favoring Ph.D.'s for full-time positions.

2. The thirty-two multiple-choice questions on the faculty evaluation instrument had to do with the following categories: the instructor's presentation of material (25 percent); the written course materials (22 percent); the course syllabus (16 percent); the instructor's encouragement of students (9 percent); the instructor's feedback or availability (9 percent); the student's own performance (19 percent).

3. Larry Cuban, *How Scholars Trumped Teachers: Change without Reform in University Curriculum, Teaching, and Research, 1890–1990* (New York: Teachers College Press, 2000); Derek C. Bok, *Our Underachieving Colleges: A Candid Look at How Much Students Learn and Why They Should be Learning More* (Princeton, N.J.: Princeton University Press, 2006).

4. Lee S. Shulman, "Those Who Understand: Knowledge Growth in Teaching," *Educational Researcher* 15, no. 2 (February 1986): 4–14.

5. Pat Hutchings and Lee Shulman, "The Scholarship of Teaching: New Elaborations, New Developments," *Change Magazine* 31 (1999): 10–15.

6. W. Norton Grubb and others, *Honored but Invisible: An Inside Look at Teaching in Community Colleges* (New York: Routledge, 1999), 276.

7. Describing the norms of postsecondary teaching, Randy Bass points out, "In one's teaching, a 'problem' is something you don't want to have, and if you have one, you probably want to fix it. . . . Asking [a colleague] about a problem in [his or her] teaching would probably seem like an accusation." Indeed, a problem in teaching tends to become a sign of individual inadequacy (student's or instructor's), something that calls for blame, judgment, and correction. Proposing an alternative understanding of teaching practice, he asks, "How might we make the problematization of teaching a matter of regular communal discourse? How might we think of teaching practice, and the evidence of student learning, as problems to be investigated, analyzed, represented, and debated?" Randy Bass, "The Scholarship of Teaching: What's the Problem?" *Inventio: Creative Thinking about Learning and Teaching* 1 (1999), accessed Feb. 12, 2009, at http://www.doit.gmu.edu/Archives/feb98/randy-bass.htm.

8. Mary T. Huber and Pat Hutchings, *The Advancement of Learning: Building the Teaching Commons* (San Francisco: Jossey-Bass, 2005).

APPENDIX

1. For further details on the study, see *Defending the Community College Equity Agenda,* ed. Thomas R. Bailey and Vanessa Smith Morest (Baltimore: Johns Hopkins University Press, 2006), 20–24.

ACKNOWLEDGMENTS

The generous support and guidance that I encountered during each stage of this project arrived in many forms and from innumerable sources. Indeed, no amount of thanks could express my appreciation to everyone who has contributed to my thinking on the topic or to the writing of the book.

My primary thanks must go those who participated in the four research studies that form the basis for *The College Fear Factor*. I am sincerely grateful to the many faculty members, administrators, and students who spent time interviewing with me. Even more critical was the generosity of the seven professors who not only graciously invited me into their classrooms for a full semester, but also agreed to spend additional time in many interviews—whether formal or informal, short or long.

Although I conducted the classroom studies as the sole researcher, I was part of a larger research team for the two studies conducted by the Community College Research Center at Teachers College, Columbia University. I am indebted to all the contributing researchers for those two projects, but I am particularly thankful to those responsible for the design and organization of the studies. For both the National Field Study and the Advanced Technological Education Projects, Tom Bailey and Vanessa Smith Morest deserve special mention in that regard.

More recently, I have benefited from the support of my departmental colleagues at Seton Hall University, all of whom have been an important resource in my thinking about college teaching.

In drafting the manuscript for this book, I benefited at an early stage from the perceptive comments of Norton Grubb, who helped me clarify my thinking and hone my argument. Amanda Cox, Martin Finkelstein, Andrea Soonachan, and Maika Watanabe also provided crucial assistance by reading repeated drafts. The external reviewers helped considerably, offering key insights about the structure and accessibility of the text.

Finally, special acknowledgment goes to my editor Elizabeth Knoll, who shepherded the writing of the book with precise feedback and gentle prodding at critical points. I found it delightful to work with her.

I am sincerely thankful to all who helped.

Index